African Americans

Frederick Douglass

African

Americans

A PORTRAIT

Richard A. Long

Foreword
Maya Angelou

Crescent Books
New York • Avenel, New Jersey

Dedicated to my sister, and to my sisters

Acknowledgements: An honor roll of historians: W.E.B. Du Bois, Carter G. Woodson, Charles Wesley, Rayford Logan, Benjamin Quarles, John Hope Franklin; Maya Angelou for enthusiastic support; Sara Hollis, Caroyln Clarke, Veta Goler for indispensable assistance.

Evelyn Ashford, Olympic medalist

Facing previous page: Dr Martin Luther King

Random House
New York • Toronto • London • Sydney • Auckland

Editors: Lorraine Dickey, Anne Johnson
Production: Hugh Allan
Design: Peter Bennett
Picture Research: Julia Hanson

Copyright © 1985, 1993 Multimedia Books Ltd

ISBN 0–517–08792–8

10 9 8 7 6 5 4 3 2 1

This edition first published in the United Kingdom 1993 by Prion, an imprint of Multimedia Books Limited, 32–34 Gordon House Road, London NW5 1LP.

Published in the US by Crescent Books, distributed by Outlet Book Company, Inc., a Random House Company, 40 Engelhard Avenue, New Jersey 07001.

Filmset by August Filmsetting, Haydock, St Helens
Origination by J Film Process, Thailand
Printed in Italy by New Interlitho

CONTENTS

FOREWORD

MAYA ANGELOU

In 1985, the first edition of this book arrived on the literary scene like an idea whose time had come. Decades had passed since the last pictorial history of African Americans had been published, and there was a needful space waiting for it as wide as African beaches and as deep as the Middle Passage. Given that a traveler proceeds best toward a destination when he is aware of his point of origin, in 1985 too many young Black men and women had been enchanted by the facile pictures and the infantile dialogue of television sitcoms, and they were, at the same time, bludgeoned with realistic, vivid acts of violence and mindless brutalities on the evening news. So, Black youth were desperately in need of a book like this, a visually compelling story of Africans in the Diaspora from the mid-15th century to the mid-1980's.

Richard Long wrote with intelligence and grace, and the brief biographies of notable African Americans were easily accessible to the young minds. The photographs were not only wonderful, but many were rare and seldom seen before.

Young men and women, teenagers, and men and women of maturity have all found great benefit in this book. There is another group, however, for whom the boon was even greater and for whom the book was much more important.

A dramatic and telling encounter occurs and recurs each school day opening in the United States: A Black child and a white child enter the first grade class, their outer clothing may differ and their facility with standard English may differ, but for the purposes of my speculation, let us say that each is endowed with the same amount of natural intelligence. The white child is no less befuddled by the new physical environment than the Black child, and the Black child is no less fearful on that first day of being removed from his familiar surroundings than the white child, but miraculously they survive their trauma. At the end of the day something critical has happened which commences a separation between the white child and the Black child that is likely to grow into a chasm. When they entered the school, the portraits on the walls looked like the white child, resembled the white child's father and mother and grandfather and grandmother. The white child is not aware of this undergirding, but most

assuredly he is informed that it is alright to look the way he looks. The Black child does not get that underpinning, but is equally oblivious as the white child. Without being aware of having received a lesson, by day's end he knows that he looks "strange", "odd", "other". No one on the walls resembles his grandfather or father or mother or grandmother.

In the classroom, when our two prototypes open their school books and see the drawings of "mommy and daddy", which are easily recognizable to the white child, and somewhat strange to the Black child. The events noted in the book are more easily recognizable to the white child and less to the Black child. "Mother and Dad and Dick and Jane load the station wagon, for they are going camping," etc. At the end of a week the Black child has had little or no confirmation that he is "alright". He has not been informed that his people have been present in any of the events which the real people participate in. If his shoulders sag at the end of the month, who notices? At the end of a semester, if his grades are noticeably beneath his schoolmates, who would ever believe that unfortunate circumstance was caused by the absence of Black faces in the corridor and Black families in the textbooks? Yet, the Black child and the white child have been changed, sometimes for life, by those absences.

A book like this is not only important, its presence may be imperative if our children, Black and white, are to be disabused of the prevailing ignorance that would inform them that Blacks have done nothing, suffered nothing, achieved nothing, hence are nothing.

I am not only happy and honored to write a few words of introduction to this book, called *African Americans: A Portrait*, I commend the editor and the publisher and all aspiring writers who wish to add to the scant, but important archive that lists, bemoans, and celebrates the negative and positive aspects of our history. We do not need a romantic, non-factual account of our history which would have us believe that Blacks have done nothing wrong and everything right. No, not at all. What we need is a true account of our history. A people without a history cannot be assured that they will have a future. We need *African Americans: A Portrait* a hundred times over for the sake of those who went before, for our sake, and – oh my God – for the sake of the children.

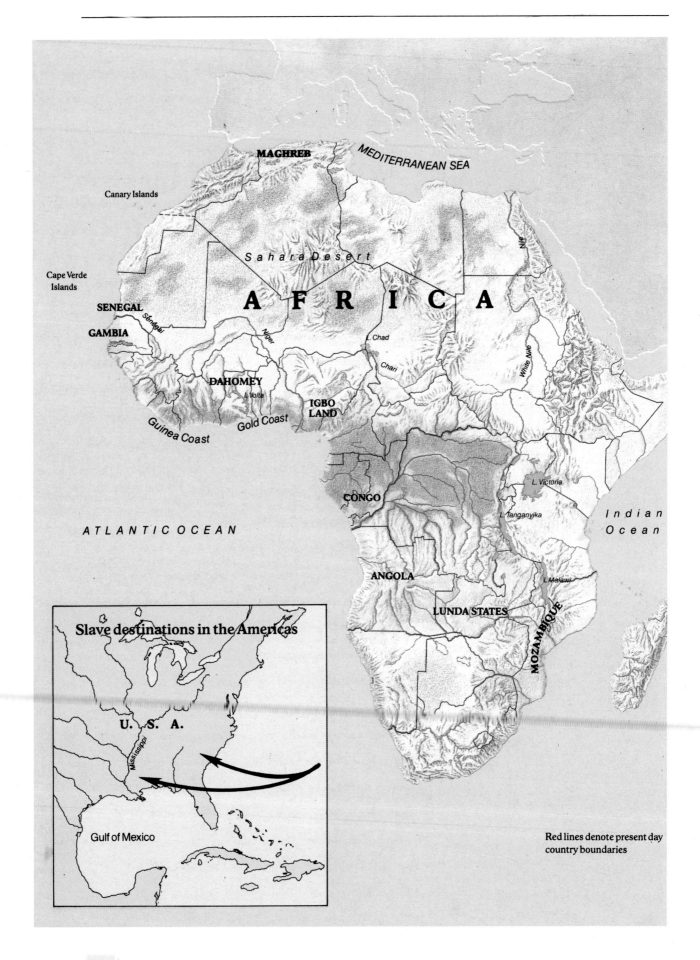

MEDITERRANEAN SEA

MAGHREB

Canary Islands

Sahara Desert

Cape Verde
Islands

A F R I C A

SENEGAL

GAMBIA

Senegal

Niger

L. Chad

Chari

Nile

White Nile

DAHOMEY

L. Volta

IGBO
LAND

Guinea Coast

Gold Coast

ATLANTIC OCEAN

CONGO

L. Victoria

L. Tanganyika

*Indian
Ocean*

ANGOLA

LUNDA STATES

L. Malawi

MOZAMBIQUE

Slave destinations in the Americas

U. S. A.

Mississippi

Gulf of Mexico

Red lines denote present day
country boundaries

CHAPTER I

SLAVERY'S END, FREEDOM'S DAWN

Below: African men, women and children were led away from their homelands – in some instances by Arab slavers as this picture indicates.

Blacks were part of the history of the New World long before the slave population of the Southern plantations made them the largest minority in the Thirteen Colonies. In the sixteenth century, the Spanish and Portuguese settlers – who came as harsh conquerors – quickly learned that Africans could adapt to the hot Caribbean islands and humid lowlands of South America. They were already familiar with the economic advantages of slavery through its introduction into Portugal in the mid-fifteenth century, following the exploration of the west coast of Africa by the great Portuguese navigators; and the Spaniards imported slaves in such large numbers that Black Africans became the majority population in some of the Caribbean islands, notably in what used to be called Hispaniola (Haiti and the Dominican Republic today).

The British, French, and Dutch took their turn at conquest, settlement, and exploitation of the New World in the seventeenth century – frequently warring with the Spanish and Portuguese and among themselves in the process. The British won out to establish themselves immovably on the east coast of the North American mainland and on some of the Caribbean islands. Shiploads of slaves began to arrive in Virginia in 1619, only 12 years after the first successful settlement there – not surprising since the British slave traders were the most active and aggressive of all, even to gaining the exclusive license to import slaves into the Spanish colonies. Again the Blacks, unfortunately for themselves, proved adaptable to plantation work and conditions so that, by the end of the seventeenth century, the prosperity of the Southern British settlements was totally tied to the institution of slavery.

Slavery was not unknown in the northern colonies in the earliest days, but the industrial development of that region called for a different kind of workforce. Slavery simply died out naturally, causing no social or political *upheaval*.

The Southern dependence on slave labor and the continuation of slavery until the later decades of the nineteenth century perhaps give a slightly distorted picture of how

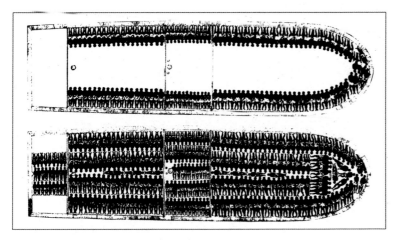

Above: Appallingly cramped and unhygienic conditions on board ship led to the deaths of many slaves. This plan of a slave ship shows the inhuman packing of Black Africans into the holds of such ships.

Below: This early engraving shows slaves being brought aboard a ship destined for North America.

many people were actually enslaved in the United States. In *The Atlantic Slave Trade: A Census* (1969), Philip Curtin estimated that approximately 470,000 Africans were brought into North America during the entire period of the slave trade – only 4.5 percent of the total numbers sent to the Americas as a whole. Of the rest, nearly 50 percent were taken by slaveholders in South America and 42 percent by owners in the Caribbean.

After the British outlawed the slave trade in 1807, some illegal importation persisted in North America so the British took the next step of making slavery itself illegal in 1833. But this decree only affected their colonies and by then the United States had long been independent, so its southern states went their own way as a stronghold of slavery. The slave population increased by natural reproduction rather than by importation of new peoples.

Who were the enslaved Black Africans? Their homelands ranged from the coasts of present-day Mozambique in the southeast to Senegal and The Gambia in the northwest – in other words, almost the whole of Black Africa. Most of them came from areas in the west and central parts of Africa and mainly from five regions within this area. Using the names of the modern countries, the five are Angola-Zaire, Nigeria, Ghana, Senegal-The Gambia, and the Ivory Coast-Liberia. The ethnic groups who inhabited these regions and who were tranplanted to the New York included the Wolof, Mandingo, Kru, Bambara, Akan, Fon, Yoruba, Ibo, and various Kongo peoples.

All they had of their own was their music, stories, religion, and dance.

These sustained them through the terrible trauma of being uprooted, transported clear across the world, and plunged into forced labor as slaves. And with many changes and adaptations, their culture seeped into the wider society around them to influence and change the United States and the rest of the world.

Black Folk-Rural Culture

While it is true that the historical presence of Blacks in the North American colonies began in 1619, we have little evidence as to their cultural presence at this time. It is most likely that in the first hundred years of life in the New World, small groups of Blacks interacted very closely with small groups of Europeans and that there arose a farmholders' culture similar to that of the colonizing Europeans. But, beginning around 1700, the numbers of Blacks coming to the North American colonies increased dramatically and this growth gave birth to an entirely new cultural structure, the first that can be called Black American.

Known as the Folk-Rural Culture, it was rooted in the conditions found in eighteenth-century plantation society and the adaptations Africans made to slavery as a way of life. The Folk-Rural Culture probably had taken distinctive form by the time of the American Revolution and it persisted in rural areas until the twentieth century.

The people who developed it are mute as individuals but we can perceive them as members of a collective: day by day, month by month, year by year, they worked out a way to survive the stringent, often brutal, demands of slave life. They did this by filling in all those human spaces that were not taken up or closely

Below: Religion – along with music, stories, and dance – helped to sustain the slaves through the trauma of transportation. These plantation slaves attend a religious meeting with their master's family.

monitored by their owners – and they turned naturally to religion, folk music, storytelling and other verbal arts, dance, and folkcraft. They also kept a hold on traditional healing and food practises.

Folk-Rural Religion

Questions of what Africans have taken from the Christianity that prevailed in North America, and what they have brought to it, are still open to debate. Certainly in the early rural world they were exposed to the fiery rhetoric of intinerant preachers and the wild emotionalism of fundamentalist congregations. Staid churchgoing, as in the cities, was for the ruling elite.

The African societies from which the slaves came were permeated by religious feeling and practise, and this religious background has to be seen as a source of emotional strength during the initial trauma of enslavement. One of the main elements of all the African religions was a great sense of the supernatural, a constant awareness of spirits, deities, and superhuman beings as always present. These beings of the other world had to be appeased, placated, pleased, won over. It was beyond an ordinary person to manage this, so a number of religious specialists assumed responsibility who were adept in a wide range of skills and practises designed to maintain harmony with the supernatural. There were also many rituals, some regular and some special, involving active participation of the larger community and generally characterized by song and dance. Both when an individual consulted a specialist and when the whole community observed a ritual, trance or possession might occur. These states were usually perceived as indicating the actual entrance of a god or goddess into the body of a person to offer advice, to bring purification, or to give a warning.

In all African cultures, a great deal of spoken lore has to do with religious life, including the supernatural. Unlike some of the rites, these stories and legends were not the exclusive property of the religious specialists, and a number of community members learned and retold them from generation to generation.

However, the slaves were not allowed their own religion, which was not considered a religion at all by the Europeans. They were therefore *Christianized*, sometimes grudgingly and largely in the hope of making them accept their place by learning the Christian precepts of meekness, temperance, and respect for those who gave the orders. It was out of a meld of these African and Christian teachings that the religion of the Folk-Rural Culture came.

It was influenced by a wave of Protestant evangelism which swept through the North American colonies at this time, and was most affected by the form embraced by the rural South. This revivalism is closely linked with the name of George Whitefield, an English evangelist who made the first of seven preaching trips to the colonies in 1738. He concentrated mainly on Georgia, but traveled throughout the South on and off for the next 32 years. Having been barred from the pulpits of the established Church of England in his homeland, he had introduced the open-air meeting there. Huge crowds attended. Whitefield brought this style of meeting – and his emotional and hypnotic style of sermonizing – to the South and

called to him all who would listen, regardless of denomination or sect.

So we find the religion of the Black Folk-Rural phase, like Whitefield's revivalism, marked by great intensity of group feeling, suggesting an amalgam of African community ritual and emotional Protestantism. Spirit possession, which was one of the tenets of African religion, was accepted by the revivalists, as long as it was the Holy Spirit.

Highly coordinated and rhythmic congregational singing, along with hand and foot movement, were also a feature of revivalist meetings. Such responses were customary for the blacks and were acceptable to the white community – as long as bodily movement fell just short of dance, which was condemned by the evangelic churches.

The most religious among the Black slave community took to re-telling the Bible stories, the history of Israel, and the experiences of Jesus and the disciples as an everyday practise. This suggests a merging of African verbal art with the evangelistic style of Christian preaching, which made constant use of simple recitations from the Bible.

The religion of the Folk-Rural Culture overall was wide-reaching, embracing, and sustaining of the individual and the community. Even so, it is important to bear in mind that not all were equally religious. In every slave community there were some who showed absolute distaste for all of it.

Folk-Rural Music

In Africa, music played a part not only in nearly all of the public observances of religion but also in virtually every other aspect of life too: work, play, conflict resolution,

Below: A prayer meeting held in secret in Washington D.C., 1862.

memory games, for example. In short, music occupied a vital role in daily life. Each cultural group had a range of musical styles and conventions, as well as a good number of musical instruments.

The musical domain of African ethnic groups was a web of intertwined genius, talent, and responsibility. Every community had some members without musical talent or inclination; these were the spectators. And each community, too, had active participants – musical leaders, instrumentalists, and, more rarely, musical creators. The training of leaders, instrumentalists, and creators was long and strenuous, beginning in early childhood. In some cultures, the instrumentalists came only from certain families or classes although, considering how important music was, it is surprising that these hereditary instrumentalists did not necessarily occupy high rank or command esteem.

The kidnapping of Africans for slavery in North America meant the transfer of people who had belonged to musical cultures and musical communities unlike any known, or even conceivable, to European societies. Their music gave the ravaged Africans an important ingredient for adapting to and regulating the hostile environment and circumstances of their new life. Since their traditional instruments were no longer available and could only occasionally be duplicated in the new lands they were taken to, they were forced to rely more on vocal music, especially in North America. Percussion effects were created by using hands and feet.

Transplanted Africans in North America absorbed some of the hymn music of Protestanism, but they also created a second thread of religious songs from their ethnic heritage. Outside of religion, in virtually all other areas of life, they rarely heard or learned any European music, so for secular music they kept to African song styles wherever possible. In time, even secular music was influenced by the strong development of religious music.

The distinctive music known as the spiritual is regarded as the outstanding musical achievement of Folk-Rural Culture. James Weldon Johnson, writer, professor, and civil rights activist, was also an acute muscial observer. He expressed his wonder and pride in his musical heritage in a famous poem, *O Black and Unknown Bards*, which begins:

O Black and unknown bards of
long ago
How came your lips to touch
the sacred fire?
How, in your darkness, did
you come to know
The power and beauty of the
minstrels' lyre?
Who first from midst his
bonds lifted his eyes?
Who first from out the still
watch, lone and long,
Feeling the ancient faith of
prophets rise
Within his dark-kept soul,
burst into song?

Johnson's eloquent questions cannot all be answered but it is obvious that the African sense of music and its musical community structure survived the transplantation to North America. And out of the new environment came the spiritual.

Blacks were originally probably not permitted to sing spirituals in public services conducted within the hearing of whites. At these times they had to sing standard hymns, to which they still brought a touch of their tradition. Commentators occasionally expressed disapproval of Black hymn singing, calling it incorrect and even irreverent. Such observers ignored the reasons why this happened – simply that Blacks found the hymns too dull and they made the songs more agreeable to their developed musical taste by exaggerating the elements of rhythm, harmony, and often˙ of melody too.

Songs known as spirituals are primarily an expression of religious faith and hope but they are not always prayerful or devotional. The Black composer-musicologist, John W. Work III, distinguishes three broad categories of spirituals: the call and response chant, the long-phrase melody, and the syncopated, segmented melody.

The first is the largest category. *Swing Low, Sweet Chariot*, one of the best-known spirituals, belongs to this group even though it is a little slower and more tranquil than most others of the type. The call and response pattern is unquestionably African and is as widely used in the non-religious song of the Folk-Rural era as it is in spirituals.

The second category, which is the rarest type, is the long-phrase spiritual. It sets up a mood of reflection and contemplation and is the only group that can properly be called sorrow songs. An example is the beloved *Deep River*.

The third category, with syncopation and segmentation, is fast and vigorous, and could more properly be called jubilee songs. *Ain't Goin' to Study War no Mo'* is a good illustration of this type.

A superb example of the long-

phrase spiritual – a true sorrow song – is *Sometimes I feel like A Motherless Child*, in which subtle melodic transitions deepen the haunting melancholy of the words:

Sometimes I feel like a motherless
child,
Sometimes I feel like a motherless
child,
Sometimes I feel like a motherless
child,
A long ways from home,
A long ways from home.

True believer,
A long ways from home,
A long ways from home.

Sometimes I feel like I'm almos'
gone,
Sometimes I feel like I'm almos'
gone,
Sometimes I feel like I'm almos'
gone;
Way up in de heab'nly lan'
Way up in de heab'nly lan'

True believer,
Way up in de heab'nly lan'
Way up in de heab'nly lan'

Sometimes I feel like a motherless
child,
Sometimes I feel like a motherless
child,
Sometimes I feel like a motherless
child,
A long ways from home.

In contrast, the joyful mood of jubilee in *Joshua Fit De Battle of Jericho* is achieved by the rollicking tempo of the melody, with its suggestion of improvization:

Joshua fit de battle ob
Jericho, Jericho, Jericho,

15

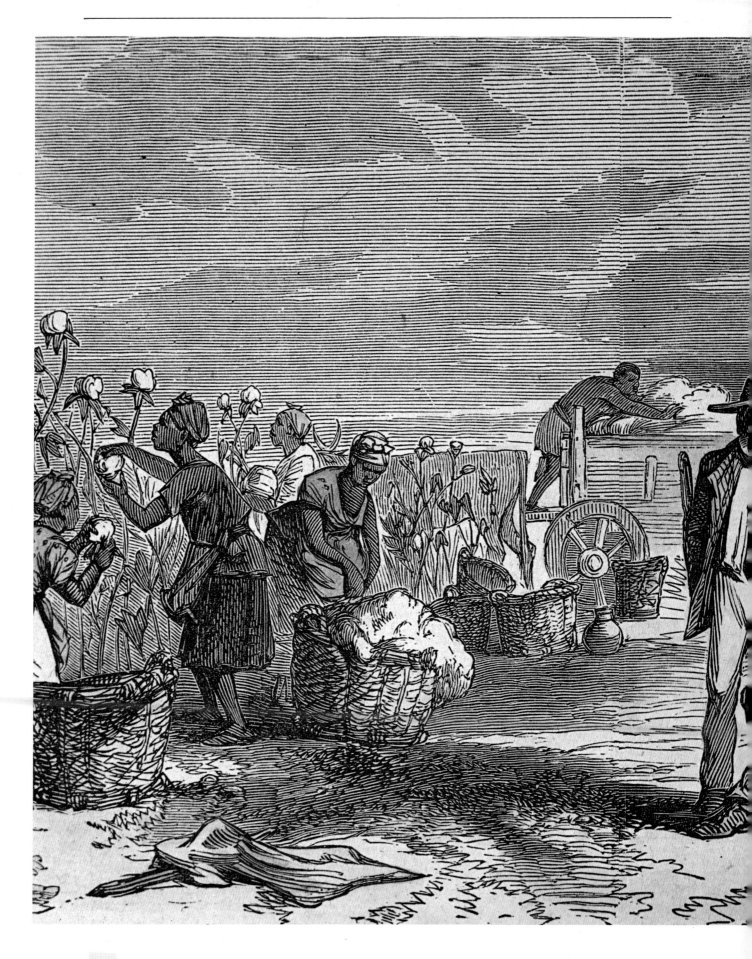

WHITE – BLACK & COLORS – FOR HAND AND MACHINE.

Joshua fit de battle ob Jericho,
An' de walls come tumblin' down.

You may talk about yo' king ob
Gideon,
You may talk about yo' king ob
Saul,
Dere's none like good ole Joshua
At de battle ob Jericho.

Up to de walls ob Jericho
He marched with spear in han'
"Go blow dem ram horns"
Joshua a cried,
"Kaze de battle am in my han'."

Den de lam' ram sheep horns begin
to blow.
Trumpets begin to soun'
Joshua commanded chillen to shout
An' de walls come tumblin' down.
Dat mornin' Joshua fit de battle ob
Jericho,
Jericho, Jericho,
Joshua fit de battle ob Jericho,
An' de walls come tumblin' down.

The call and response spiritual is
aptly illustrated by the popular *Go
Down, Moses*. Its suggestion of
opposition to slavery is cloaked in
acceptance in the scripture story:

Go down, Moses
'Way down in Egypt land,
Tell ole Pharaoh
To let my people go.

Go down, Moses
'Way down in Egypt land,
Tell ole Pharaoh,
To let my people go.

When Israel was in Egypt land:
Let my people go,
Oppressed so hard they could not
stand
Let my people go.

Go down, Moses
'Way down in Egypt land,
Tell ole Pharaoh,
To let my people go.

When spoke the Lord, bold Moses
said:
Let my people go
If not I'll smite your first born
dead,
Let my people go.

Go down, Moses
'Way down in Egypt land.
Tell ole Pharaoh,
To let my people go.

John Work once heard the call and response spiritual *Roll, Jordan, Roll* sung by a community of Afro-Americans whose ancestors went to Haiti 1824. This led him to suppose that the spiritual as a musical genre was fully formed by the late eight-

eenth century. In the long period of creation and use – extending from the Revolution to the Civil War – many spirituals ceased to be primarily religious and entered work and social life, forming a bridge between religious and secular music. The secular vocal music of the Folk-Rural Culture can be divided roughly into the two broad categories of work and social songs.

After extensive research into contemporary letters, travel writings, and other original documents, Dena J. Epstein identified several different types of work songs. These were known to be in existence after 1800, though their beginnings date from much earlier. Among them are:

Fieldwork Songs accompanying planting, hoeing, weeding, harvesting, and other farming activities using a gang of workers.

Domestic work Songs accompanying the churning of butter, spinning, basket-making, weaving, flailing rice, and the grinding of grains such as hominy.

Boating and river work Songs, generally of the call and response type, sung while doing all of the various monotonous activities associated with water transportation. This included loading and unloading ships, stoking fires, and rowing short and long boats.

Marching songs Songs for the trek. Slaves were often required to move as a group from one place to another, in an organized march formation.

Cries Songs to attract buyers. The street cry, used by urban black vendors, was related directly to the rural holler. This special cry served a variety of purposes in the country, from attracting attention or organizing a task.

Previous pages, left: Cotton production depended on slavery. By the onset of the Civil War, 2.4 million slaves were engaged in cotton production.

Previous pages, right: The illustration on this 1890s advertisement for J & P Coats Best Six-Cord Spool Cotton gives some indication of the substantial Black involvement in the cotton industry.

Below: The invention of the cotton gin in 1793 changed cotton from a minor crop to the most important export from the United States by the Civil War.

The social songs of the Folk-Rural Culture are less well documented. They included lullabies and game songs for children and adults, some of which have been preserved by performers like Bessie Jones and the Sea Island Singers. It should be recalled, though, that spirituals frequently became the songs for convivial social gatherings unrelated to prayer meeting. Similarly, work songs were often sung for pleasure and release during leisure time.

Folk-Rural Verbal Art

The verbal art of the Folk-Rural Culture has clear connections with Africa. The transition from the languages of that continent to the everyday speech of Black Americans of the era was certainly a complicated one. Though called Creole only in Louisiana, it is, like that dialect, a language based on several languages – various African tongues and southern plantation English.

The sermon of the Folk-Rural preacher has long been the object of study and respect. James Weldon Johnson, who immortalized it in *God's Trombones*, wrongly believed at the time that it was a dying tradition. The Black preacher descends in a direct line from the African storyteller, and has done for listeners in America what the storyteller did for his audience. Both are available at a given time and place, the preacher in the church on Sunday and the storyteller in the village square on market day. Each dramatizes the tale that is told and the tale is always a traditional one, more or less well known to the audience. The audience in both cases not only empathizes with the recital, but shows feeling through voice and body. So Africa was recreated in the Folk-Rural Culture under the unsuspecting mantle of Christianity.

There are three rhythmic styles in the sermon tradition – emphatic, legato, and syncopated – and the preacher draws on symbols and images outside the realms of the English language and the tradition of Euro-American sermons. The language used in spirituals and secular songs is important as words, but is most important as a song. There is poetry in the spiritual, but it owes its power to its union with the music and there is a danger that separating the words from the music will reduce full appreciation of them. It is, however, the only possible way to show the words as poetry.

Along with scripture stories told and retold by the gifted preacher-storyteller, secular animal tales, with their source in Africa, were also part of the verbal art of the Folk-Rural

Below: Emancipation became an extremely hot issue – this Abolitionist meeting being broken up in Tremont Temple, Boston, in 1858 was indicative of the high feelings surrounding the issue.

Culture. It is interesting that the largest cache of these animal tales known to the public are those recounted by Joel Chandler Harris in the *Uncle Remus Tales*. The frame in which Harris placed the stories – the old ex-slave telling them to a young white boy in a happy plantation setting – gave a false picture of them as simple children's tales. In their real setting within the Folk-Rural Culture, they are examples of a sophisticated verbal art related by a virtuoso to an audience of devotees.

Folk-Rural Dance

Dance in Africa is, of course, very closely tied to music, so it follows that its community pattern is very similar: there are the spectators, the active participants, the specialists, and the leaders.

Dancing itself was varied. There were general dances in which a large part of the community took part, and others in which only one specific group participated – young women, or young men, or older women, for example. And there were highly specialized and intricate performances by single dancers, others by well-rehearsed groups as well as competitive exhibitions of acrobatic skill.

In North America we hear much about the continuity of the African dance tradition among Blacks. There are even early accounts of Blacks performing dances in imitation or satire of Europeans, itself in the tradition since the dances of Africa are frequently imitations of the carriage and movement of certain birds and animals, and are often satiric as well. So continuity did exist, although mainly in general community dancing, for, in the slave condition, what opportunity would there be for the development of dance specialists and of leaders?

Something else worked against the African tradition of dance in the Folk-Rural Culture: the constant tension caused by the views of the Christian evangelism to which the Blacks had been converted. In their own customs, the dance had been both religious and secular, both ritual and recreational. In Protestant fundamentalism, all kinds of dancing was generally regarded as a moral laxity that could only lead to evil and sin. Torn between dance as a vital part of life and dance as a guidepost to damnation, the slave community was divided. To add to the confusion, some planters actively encouraged dancing as a palliative.

Acute observers of plantation life report that many slave communities contained two distinct groups, frequently in conflict and never in harmony: the praying band and the

Below left: The invoice of a sale of Black slaves dated 1835, signed by John W. Pittman of Georgia.

Below right: A slave auction in Virginia around 1860.

dancing band. Probably the practise of dancing for exhilaration and release in their few leisure hours was widespread. In any case, this division in sentiment over the role of dance is reflected in later periods of Afro-American culture.

Slavery and Cotton

The plantation was the birthplace of the Folk-Rural Culture. There were roughly two zones of plantation development in the mid-eighteenth century: coastal and riverine Virginia for tobacco growing, and coastal South Carolina for rice and indigo. Then came the Cotton Kingdom in the early nineteenth century – and a wide extension of plantations. The Folk-Rural Culture extended to the Cotton Kingdom through the internal slave trade, the older plantations selling off some of their slaves to the labor-hungry new plantations in Alabama, Mississippi, and, later,

Texas. *Uncle Tom's Cabin*, written in 1852, describes a well-known practise when it talks about selling slaves "down South".

Until 1793, cotton had been a minor crop in the American South but the invention of the cotton gin in that year, which separated the seeds from the fibre mechanically, was a revolutionary event in the history of the United States. And it changed slavery from a dying institution to the central economic and political issue in American life from the adoption of the Constitution to the Civil War. In 1793 the United States produced 10,000 bales of cotton, in 1800 production was 100,000 bales. As a result, the price of slaves doubled. By the time of the Civil War, 60 percent of· the slave population of four million was engaged in cotton production – and cotton accounted for two-thirds of the value of exports from the United States.

The extension of the Cotton Kingdom meant the maintenance and extension of Black slavery for economic interests – in the South for growing cotton and in the North for manufacturing cotton goods. All defenses, apologies, and rationalization of slavery are based on this bedrock of economic interest.

The growth of Abolition sentiment in the North was seen by the South as a threat to its way of life. Slaveholders tried a few measures to improve the system but refused to give it up. Secession, the formation of the Confederacy, and armed defiance were the most traumatic efforts of the Southern elite to preserve the institution of slavery.

Citadin Black Culture

The overwhelming majority of Blacks in the colonies and early

Below: The extension of the Cotton Kingdom meant the maintenance of Black slavery for economic reasons – in the South, gracious plantation houses like this one along the Mississippi were only made possible by the sweat of slaves.

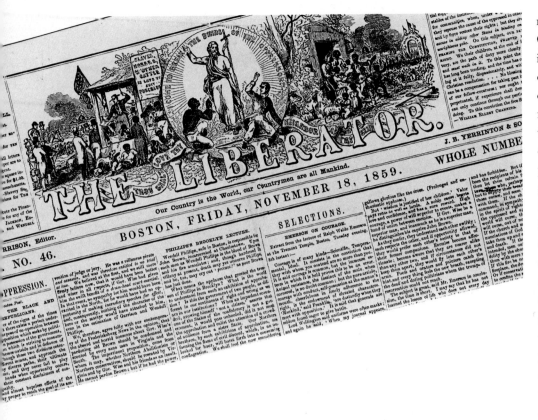

republic were part of the Folk-Rural Culture, but there were Blacks living in the cities. Their life was naturally quite different to those in rural areas, conforming in varying degrees to the norms found there, and almost from the start they were marked off as a distinctive cultural group through prejudice, discrimination, and segregation. We may speak of a Citadin Black Culture which emerges in Philadelphia, Boston, and other cities in the eighteenth century and continued down to the twentieth century. The Black community was made up of artisans and laborers with a scattering of teachers, ministers, and other professionals. In the period before the Civil War, the overwhelming group interest of Citadin Culture in the North was the Abolition of slavery.

Citadin Culture, understandably different, also existed in the South in cities like Richmond and Charleston, where it was closely entwined with the Southern way of life. For example, some Southern Blacks were listed as slaveholders, and while in most cases this was only a legal fiction, accounted for by a Black's purchase of his wife or children from bondage, in some instances it was an actual owner-slave relationship.

Abolitionists – White and Black

The language of freedom that was so popular during the American Revolution brought the institution of slavery into sharp focus. The Second Continental Congress, which adopted the Declaration of Independence, took no stand on slavery, but there is evidence that many of its members did not press the point mostly because they felt that slavery was a dying institution. In fact, the

Above: William Lloyd Garrison launched the abolitionist newspaper, *The Liberator*, in 1931.

Facing page: Frederick Douglass was made instantly famous by the spare and sure eloquence of his 1845 Narrative, in which he gives the circumstances of his life as a slave. He went on to become the most powerful and representative spokesman for Blacks in the period during the Civil War.

original draft of the Declaration attacked the slave trade as a deplorable British institution, but this was deleted before the final signatures were appended.

The Declaration of Independence and the Revolution ran side by side with an organized abolitionist movement that continued throughout the century. In 1775 the Pennsylvania Society for Promoting the Abolition of Slavery was founded in Philadelphia; Societies were formed in other cities and states in succeeding years and in 1794 a national group came into being.

The early abolitionists took a soft approach. Their program advocated compensation for slaveholders for slaves they willingly freed and was generally gradualist and low-key. It eventually petered out.

A new abolitionism appeared in the wake of the extension of slavery, which had not been halted by the uneasy Missouri Compromise of 1820. In 1829 David Walker's *Appeal*, with its argument that slavery was against the will of God, created havoc in the slaveholding states of the South. This was bad enough, but his call for resistance to slavery was intolerable to the ruling elite. In 1831 Nat Turner's Rebellion in Southampton County, Virginia, seemed a fulfilment of David Walker's call. The reaction in the South was even harsher treatment of the slaves.

In the same year as the Turner Rebellion, William Lloyd Garrison launched the abolitionist newspaper, *The Liberator*, in Boston. Garrison, journalist and reformer, published his *Thoughts on African Colonization* in 1832 in which he rejected the African colonization program supported by many white Americans

both in the North and South. He was also instrumental in organizing the American Anti-Slavery Society in 1833.

Among other outspoken supporters of abolition were Henry Ward Beecher, Lydia Maria Childs, Cassius Marcellus Clay – one of the few white Southern abolitionists – and Sarah and Angelina Grimke, sisters who were born in South Carolina and moved to the North to work in the anti-slavery cause. Other outstanding abolitionists included Edward Everett Hale and Wendell Phillips, who were both among the greatest American orators of their time; the poets John Greenleaf Whittier and James Russell Lowell; and Thomas Wentworth Higginson, who was to be the colonel of a Black regiment in the Civil War and mentor of the poet Emily Dickinson later in life. In 1837, Elijah Lovejoy became a martyr to the abolitionist cause when a pro-slavery mob killed him while he was defending the press on which he printed the *Alton Observer* in Alton, Illinois. His brother Owen, who witnessed the murder, later served in the US Congress from 1857 to 1864. He was a strong supporter of Abraham Lincoln.

Garrison was the dominant figure in the anti-slavery movement until 1840, when a crisis over his leadership caused a split. The separation occurred because Garrison took positions that antagonized or alienated some of his associates and they considered that his interests were unrelated, or even hamful, to the central issue of abolition. For example, Garrison was highly critical of the churches, considering them allies of the slaveholders; he supported women's rights, and was a pacifist and active in the temperance movement. The

Previous pages: The coming of the Civil War was welcomed by those in bondage and many Blacks found their way into the Unionist army. Here a troop of Black soldiers storm Fort Wagner in 1863.

Below and facing page: Harriet Beecher Stowe's Novel and play, *Uncle Tom's Cabin*, was influenced by the slave narrative of Father Henson. Left is a handbill from the play, while right is a list indicating just how popular the book became all over the English-speaking world.

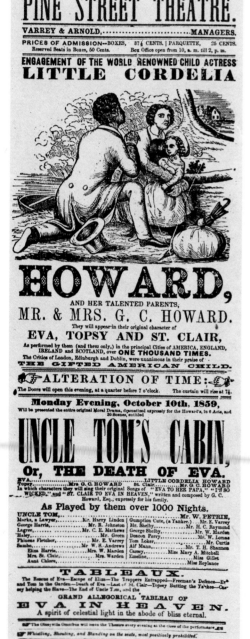

splinter group, which wished to focus exclusively on abolition, called itself the American and Foreign Anti-Slavery Society.

Many former slaves came to the fore as eloquent pleaders for the freedom of their people. The greatest of these was Frederick Douglass.

Henry Highland Garnet, like Douglass born a slave on the Eastern shore of Maryland, emerged as the most radical of the Black abolitionists. His strong *Address to the Slaves of the United States of America* was rejected by a slight majority at a National Convention of Blacks meeting in Buffalo in 1843, but he published it in 1848. The closing paragraph called for out-and-out resistance to slavery itself.

Slave Narratives

As part of the abolitioinist campaign, which intensified towards the 1840s, a number of narratives of slave life began to appear. The slave narrative is an important genre of American writing, unique in its character and gripping in its power. The genuine emotions of horror and resentment aroused at the time they were published have continued to the present day and have perhaps somewhat screened their value as social history and biography.

It is now recognized that the slave narratives written and published in the two decades before the Civil War present a true and accurate picture of the lives of most Blacks under slavery. In the case of narratives dictated by Blacks unable to write, it is accepted that those who took them down were faithful to the facts and to the spirit of the narrator.

The accounts of slave life written in the years after Emancipation form part of a larger literary undertaking

and are not considered slave narratives as such. This is true, for instance, of Frederic Douglass' *Life and Times of Frederick Douglass*, published in 1881.

Another class of writings, also sometimes wrongly called slave narratives, are reminiscences collected in the twentieth century of Blacks born prior to Emancipation. The largest group of these accounts was collected in the 1930s by the Work's Progress Administration (WPA), the Federal employment program that was part of Roosevelt's New Deal. Most of the collectors were well-educated whites who wrote down the reminiscences as told to them by former slaves, well advanced in age by then.

While these reminiscences have interest and value, it should be remembered that most of those interviewed were very young at the time of Emancipation, and that over 60 years had passed since their direct experience of slavery. Nevertheless, the folk character of these recollections have made them better known than more formal slave narratives.

In the 15 years after the appearance of the *Narrative of the Life of Frederic Douglass, An American Slave* in 1845, at least 30 important slave narratives were written. Douglass' is no doubt the most outstanding of all, but five others are of special quality.

William Wells Brown told his story in *Narrative of William Wells Brown, A Fugitive Slave* (1847). After escaping to the North, Brown achieved prominence in abolitionist circles second only to that of Douglass. He later lived in England and France for five years, also writing an account of his activities in those countries. Brown wrote a novel,

AUTHOR'S EDITIONS.

Below: Facsimile of letter sent by the slave Thomas Duckett to his former master:

Mr. Bigelow. – Dear Sir, – I write to let you know how I am getting along. I have not had one hour to go outside the place since I have been on it. I written to hear from you all. Mr. Bigelow, I hope you will not forget me. You know it was not my fault that I am here. I hope you will name me to Mr. Geden, Mr. Chaplin, Mr. Bailey, to help me out of it. I believe that if they would make the least move to it that it could be done. I long to hear from my family how they are getting along. You will please to write to me just to let me know how they are getting along. You can write to me.

I remain your humble servant,
THOMAS DUCKET.

Clotel, and a play, *The Escape*, both portrayals of slavery.

The year after Brown's book came *Narrative of the Life and Adventures of Henry Bibb, An American Slave*. Bibb was born around 1815 and lived as a slave on several plantations before escaping in 1837. He made four trips to the South in efforts to free his family.

Narrative of the Life of Henry Box Brown (1849) and *Running a Thousand Miles for Freedom or The Escape of William and Ellen Craft from Slavery* (1860) are two of the more sensational stories. Brown took his middle name from the fact that he had himself shipped from Virginia to Philadelphia in a box – and lived to tell the tale. Ellen Craft disguised herself as a young planter and her husband traveled with her as the "master's" servant.

The story of Father Henson is a special one. It was his character that influenced Harriet Beecher Stowe's portrayal of Uncle Tom in her world-shaking abolitionist novel, *Uncle Tom's Cabin or Life among the Lowly* (1852). His own narrative, *Truth Stranger than Fiction: Father Henson's Story of His Own Life* (1858), reveals an extraordinary character who saved more than 100 people from slavery.

The writers of the slave narratives were among the most admirable Americans of their time. They struggled against the indignity and oppression of slavery and escaped. And after they did, they devoted themselves to the enlightenment and liberation of their people.

The Fifties and the Civil War

In the 1850s, the big planters who supplied the textile mills of the North and of England had their eyes on ever greater profits. Slavery was essential to this aim, and the slaveholders grew bolder in their determination to preserve it – there was even open agitation for the reopening of the African slave trade in the Congress of the United States. It was not enough that Congress had passed the Fugitive Slave Law in 1850, which encouraged Southerners to pursue their slaves to Northern cities, and which made many Blacks flee over the border to Canada to ensure their safety.

In 1854, again yielding to pressure by slaveholders, Congress passed the Kansas-Nebraska Act. This in effect repealed the Missouri Compromise of 1820, which had decreed that slavery would not extend North of a 36°30′ latitude.

In 1857, the clock was set back for Black civil rights. The Supreme Court ruled by a vote of seven to two that Dred Scott, a Black who was suing for his freedom on the grounds that he had lived in territory where slavery was forbidden, had no right to sue, and that "no Black could be a citizen of any state, regardless of his status." The court went beyond the specific matter before it, to retroactively deny Congress the legislative right to vote through the Missouri Compromise.

It is against this background that the events leading up to the Civil War must be seen – and against this background it can be seen that the war was indeed about slavery.

In 1861, following the firing on Fort Sumpter, Frederick Douglass wrote a fiery editorial *Nemesis*.

At last our proud Republic is overtaken. Our National Sin has found us out. The National Head is bowed down, and our face is mantled with shame and confusion. No foreign arm is made bare for our chastisement. No distant monarch, offended at our freedom and prosperity, has plotted our destruction; no envious tyrant has prepared for our necks his oppressive yoke. Slavery has done it all. Our enemies are those of our own household. It is civil war, the worst of all wars, that has unveiled its savage and wrinkled front among us. During the last twenty years and more, we have as a nation been forging a bolt for our own national destruction, collecting and augmenting the fuel that now threatens to wrap the nation in its malignant and furious flames. We have sown the wind, only to reap the whirlwind. Against argument, against all manner of appeal and remonstrances coming up from the warm and merciful heart of humanity, we have gone on like the oppressors of Egypt, hardening our hearts and increasing the burdens of the American slave, and strengthening the arm of his guilty master, till now, in the pride of his giant power, that master is emboldened to lift rebellious arms against the very majesty of the law, and defy the power of the Government itself. In vain have we plunged our souls into new and unfathomed depths of sin, to conciliate the favor and secure the loyalty of the slaveholding class. We have hated and persecuted the Negro; we have scourged him

out of the temple of justice by the Dred Scott decision; we have shot and hanged his friends at Harper's Ferry; We have enacted laws for his further degradation, and even to expel him from the borders of some of our States; we have joined in the infernal chase to hunt him down like a beast, and fling him into the hell of slavery; we have repealed and trampled upon laws designed to prevent the spread of slavery, and in a thousand ways given our strength, our moral and political influence to increase the power and ascendancy of slavery over all departments of Government; and now, as our reward, this slaveholding power comes with sword, gun and cannon to take the life of the nation and overthrow the great American Government.

There is no more moving and telling an expression of the Blacks' view of the Civil War than this.

It is ironic that only a few days before Fort Sumpter was attacked, Douglass had agreed to make a trip to Haiti to investigate the possibility of emigration there by free Blacks, at the invitation of the Haitian government. He had always been a strong foe of emigration and repatriation schemes, but the increasingly hostile environment for Blacks in the United States, and the growing power of the slave-holders in the government, worried him into exploring the option.

The coming Civil War was not unwelcome to those in bondage. There is abundant testimony that the slaves of the South saw their way to

freedom in the armies of the North although they had little means to help themselves or the Northern cause. In fact, it is a cruel twist of fate that the South was able to remain in the field as long as it did because of its exploitation of its slaves. There was some recognition that this resource was fragile, however. After Lincoln issued the Emancipation Proclamation in 1863, many leaders of the Confederacy considered schemes for the enlistment of Blacks in their armies and for their eventual freedom. The contradictions in these ideas are plain, and nothing was done. Meantime, Blacks sought refuge behind the Union lines in greater and greater numbers throughout the war.

At the end of the war in 1865, Congress promulgated the Thirteenth Amendment to the Constitution. Slavery was abolished at last.

Above: Andrew Scott, a Black soldier who served the Union cause in the Civil War.

CHAPTER II

THE JOURNEY FORWARD

Facing page: As a major abolitionist figure, Sojourner Truth was a forceful platform speaker. A New York Slave freed at the virtual extinction of slavery in New York, 1827, she also participated in the Women's Rights Movement.

Below: Harriet Tubman (far left) with a group of slaves whom she helped to escape. As a celebrated "conductor" of the Underground Railroad, she is credited with leading 300 people to freedom, following her own escape from slavery. She served as a nurse during the Civil War.

The end of the Civil War in 1865 marks the beginning of a new cultural phase for the Black American – the Folk-Urban. In spite of hope on one side and promises on the other, the victory for the North did not mean that Blacks were immediately accepted into the mainstream of society. Their expectations of political, social, and economic advancement were obstructed by deep-rooted opposition that surfaced at every step. Federal law was on their side at least: slavery was officially ended by the Thirteenth Amendment. A Civil Rights Act, enacted by Congress in 1866, was intended to guarantee citizenship rights, and the essence of this act became the Fourteenth Amendment. The Fifteenth Amendment was passed to assure the right to vote.

The attempt to implement these amendments by some Northerners, as well as the determination to frustrate them by most Southerners, underlies the drama of Reconstruction, and the reaction and compromise of Post-Reconstruction.

The migration of Blacks to cities following the Civil War began a process which, as for all Americans, was to end in their becoming an overwhelmingly urban population by the time of World War II. The incoming rural Blacks found urban Blacks already established in the city way of life, mostly as free people, and some of them seemed to have little in common with the former slaves, even though not all of them were fully urbanized themselves.

The new city dwellers soon created a distinct phase of Black culture, which we call the Folk-Urban. Its roots lay in the Folk-Rural Culture, which continued to feed it for several decades by new arrivals from the countryside.

It was also nourished by the constant two-way traffic that took place between city and country – city folk would visit family members in the country and vice-versa. Similarly, children of city dwelleres would often be sent to the country to stay with relatives for longer or shorter periods of time.

This pattern of interaction continued until after World War II when the Folk-Rural Culture faded out except for isolated pockets.

TO BE SOLD on board the Ship Bance-Yland, on tuesday the 6 May next, at Afhley-Ferry; a cho cargo of about 250 fine healthy NEGROES, just arrived from the Windward & Rice Coaft. —The utmoft care has already been taken, and continued, to keep them danger of being infect no boat havi communi pr

CAUTION!!
COLORED PEOPLE
OF BOSTON, ONE & ALL,
You are hereby respectfully CAUTIONED and advised, to avoid conversing with the
Watchmen and Police Officers of Boston,
For since the recent ORDER OF THE MAYOR & ALDERMEN, they are empowered to act as
KIDNAPPERS
AND
Slave Catchers,
And they have already been actually employed in KIDNAPPING, CATCHING, AND KEEPING SLAVES. Therefore, if you value your LIBERTY, and the Welfare of the Fugitives among you, Shun them in every possible manner, as so many HOUNDS on the track of the most unfortunate of your race.

Above: A handbill advertising the sale of slaves contrasts with another warning for Black people to look out for kidnappers in Boston.

The Freedman's Bureau

In 1865, Congress set up a bureau to deal with the urgent problems created by the sudden emancipation of four million slaves. This agency, the Freedman's Bureau, had a massive task, which it pursued actively until 1869. Many of its executives were military officers, often helped by religious charities. They worked to establish hospitals, schools, courts, banks, and other necessary institutions. The Bureau extended help to whites as well as to Blacks, if they qualified as "refugees" under the act creating the Bureau.

During the Civil War itself there had already been a pioneering effort to help recently emancipated Blacks adjust to freedom by schooling and paid employment. This experiment took place in the federally held section of South Carolina at Port Royal and attracted teachers from the North, among them a granddaughter of the Black abolitionist James Forten.

Charlotte Forten spent two years at Port Royal and her *Journal* of that period is a fascinating and important piece of Afro-American history. In late January 1863, she went to visit Harriet Tubman, who was already a legend in her own time for her many dangerous excursions to free some 300 of her people along the "Underground Railroad". Charlotte Forten wrote of the visit:

In Beaufort we spent nearly all our time at Harriet Tubman's – otherwise "Moses". She is a wonderful woman – a real heroine. Has helped off a large number of slaves, after taking her own freedom. She told us that she used to hide them in the woods during the day and go around to get provisions for them. Once she had with her a man named Joe, for whom a reward of $1500 was offered. Frequently, in different places she found handbills exactly describing him, but at last they reached in safety the Suspension Bridge over the Falls and found themselves in Canada. Until then, she said, Joe had been very silent. In vain had she called his attention to the glory of the Falls. He sat perfectly still – moody, it seemed, and w'ld not even glance at them. But when she said, "Now we are in Canada" he sprang to his feet with a great shout, and sang and clapped his hands in a perfect delirium of joy. So when they got out, she said, and he first touched free soil, he shouted and hurrahed "as if he were crazy."

How exciting it was to hear her tell the story. And to hear her sing the very scraps of jubilant hymns that he sang. She said the ladies crowded around them, and some laughed and some cried. My own eyes were full as I listened to her – the heroic woman! A reward of $10,000 was offered for her by the Southerners, and her friends deemed it best that she sh'ld, for a time find refuge in Canada. And she did so, but only for a short time. She came back and was soon at the good brave work again. She is living in Beaufort now, keeping an eating house, but she wants to go North, and will probably do so ere long. I am glad I saw her – *very glad.*

W.E.B. Du Bois, writer, editor, and civil rights leader, wrote about the work and the many problems of the Freedman's Bureau in 1903:

> Such was the dawn of Freedom; such was the work of the Freedman's Bureau, which, summed up in brief, may be epitomized thus: for some fifteen million dollars, beside the sums spent before 1865, and the dole of benevolent societies, this Bureau set going a system of free labor, established a beginning of peasant proprietorship, secured the recognition of black freedmen before the courts of law, and founded the free common school in the South. On the other hand, it failed to begin the establishment of good-will between ex-masters and freedmen, to guard its work wholly from paternalistic methods which discouraged self-reliance, and to carry out to any considerable extent its implied promises to furnish the freedmen with land. Its successes were the result of hard work, supplemented by the aid of philanthropists and the eager striving of black men. Its failures were the result of bad local agents, the inherent difficulties of the work, and national neglect.

Reconstruction

Abraham Lincoln, who considered the states of the South to be in rebellion against the Union rather than in sucession from it, had conceived a plan for their reintegration upon the agreement of 10 percent of their population. Lincoln's plan, the so-called Presidential Reconstruction, was followed in general by President Andrew Johnson, who succeeded after his assassination. However, the ex-Confederate States wanted reintegration on their own terms, and their terms were a virtual reenslavement of the freed Blacks. They resisted the Fourteenth Amendment and devised a set of extremely harsh "Black Codes" to control the movements and activities of Blacks. They also formed terrorist organizations with names like Regulators and Jay Hawkers to keep Blacks in line.

In 1867, the radical wing of the Republican Party came into control of Congress. Unlike Lincoln, these legislators considered that the Confederate states had seceded instead of rebelled, and therefore had to be readmitted rather than reintegrated. They held that Congress could determine the conditions of readmission, and insisted on the grant of votes to Blacks as central to that readmission. After a fierce struggle with President Johnson (which included an effort to impeach him that only just failed), Congress passed the Reconstruction Act of 1867. This severe legislation is called Congressional Reconstruction and organized the ten Southern states in five miltary districts under military governors responsible for the political reorganization.

During Reconstruction, much progress was made toward making Blacks full citizens, and they were elected to State legislatures and other offices. At no time did Blacks ever control any of the ex-Confederate State governments, however, though racist propaganda posing as history has made that claim. Only a start, the Black participation in Reconstruction politics was nonetheless

Below: The Klu Klux Klan surfaced in the South after the Civil War. This drawing appeared in *Harper's Weekly* on December 19, 1868.

Above: Lynchings and mob rule became the order of the day. This early engraving shows a mob lynching a Black man in Charleston Street, New York, during riots in 1863.

basically progressive and healthy. The charge of corruption which has been made against some of the Reconstruction governments was justifiable, although it must be remembered that corruption was a general characteristic of state government in the United States at that time.

Opposition to Black participation in government became so intense in the South that it spawned the most infamous white supremist organization of them all, the Ku Klux Klan. Known as the "Invisible Empire," the Klan used terror to frighten Blacks into submission. The peak period of this first Klan was from 1869 to 1871 but both the name and the tactics were to remain a power in the South right down to the present.

Post-Reconstruction

The four years of the Civil War weigh heavily on the history of the United States; Reconstruction, which lasted three times as long, weighs equally heavily on the history of the American South. The Post-Reconstruction years, which started with the election of 1876, weigh immeasurably heavily on the history of the Blacks. The compromise of 1877 started a process of restriction and nullification of the rights of Blacks in the South which lasted for at least a hundred years – and some will claim has not ended even today.

The North had never been passionately interested in or committed to the fate of Southern Blacks, having its own fill of discrimination and prejudice. So the hardening of discriminatory law and custom in the South after 1877 went on with the tacit, and sometimes outright, approval of the North.

The compromise that brought

about the collapse of Reconstruction was the result of the disputed election between the Democratic candidate Samuel S. Tilden and the Republican Rutherford B. Hayes. Both were reform-minded governors, Tilden of New York and Hayes of Ohio. Tilden won the popular vote by a plurality of 250,000 but fell one short of a majority in the Electoral College. Congress appointed an electoral commission to solve the problem amid widespread political confusion. Southern Democrats agreed to support the Republican in return for the recall of federal troops and the administrators of Reconstruction policies from the South. This political horse-trading returned Southern Blacks to the untender mercies of their former oppressors.

Soon after the inauguration of Hayes, the troops were withdrawn and white supremacy reigned again throughout the South. Ways of getting round the Fifteenth Amendment were found in all the Southern states, and by 1885 Blacks were virtually disfranchised. Klan-type violence flourished parallel with the Age of Demagogues, which arose during the 1890s.

Mob violence and lynch law as a widely accepted behavior by whites was an especially repugnant aspect of the Reaction in the South. The tradition of a mob taking the law into their own hands to put an accused wrongdoer to death without a legal trial, usually by hanging, dated from Revolutionary days when it was used against Loyalists; later it was also employed against Indians and some whites. But in the years from 1880 to 1930, almost the sole victims of this barbaric practice were the Southern Blacks. Records kept by Tuskegee Institute reveal that over 4000 Blacks were lynched during this period – and tens of thousands of others were terrorized in the process. Southern senators successfully prevented the passing of federal anti-lynching laws for about 50 years.

The Legalization of Jim Crow

Jim Crow was the nineteenth-century American version of apartheid. Jim Crow laws ate away at the legal rights and the human dignity of Blacks in the South, imposing separation of the races as the only acceptable way of life for whites. Based on the separate but equal doctrine, Jim Crow affected every aspect of Black-white relations – at home, at work, at school, in public places, in travel, in entertainment. Segregation as a fact had long existed in the North as well as the South, but the Jim Crow laws drew an indelible color line that divided Black from white in all things and they were enshrined in the constitutions of all the Southern states in the Post-Reconstruction period.

Tennessee led the way with the first Jim Crow law in 1875, and was quickly followed by the other states of the former Confederacy. Among the early targets for the separate but equal treatment were the railroads, which had to put on special coaches for Blacks only when they reached the Jim Crow states. Following the passage of Louisiana's railroad law in 1890, a citizens' group challenged it. A test case was made of Homer Plessy, who in 1892 brought a suit after being arrested for riding on a white-only coach. The railroads secretly supported the challenger because of the enormous expense they incurred in providing separate coaches but Plessy lost in the state courts and the appeal went up to the U.S. Supreme Court. In 1896 the

Below: A Florida movie house, 1930s. Note that the rear entrance is for "colored" people.

highest court in the land ruled by a majority of eight to one that the Fourteenth Amendment, which granted citizenship rights to Blacks, did not debar separate but equal accommodations. This made the Jim Crow laws constitutional. The cost of maintaining two school systems was especially high, and whites paid not only in financial terms but also in educational terms because of the generally low standards that were the result.

John Marshall Harlan was the lone dissenter to the reactionary Supreme Court decision. Justice Harlan declared that the U.S. constitution was "color-blind" and predicted in the dissent that the Plessy case would "prove to be quite as pernicious as the decision made by the same tribunal in the Dred Scott case."

Booker T. Washington: Tuskegee and the New South

Born in Virginia about 1856, Booker Taliaferro and his family moved to Malden, West Virginia, immediately after the Civil War. There he worked in the salt and coal mines by day and attended school by night. In 1872, driven by the desire for an education, he made his way to the Hampton Normal and Agricultural Institute nearly 300 miles away by walking and hitch-hiking. His tuition was paid by a friend of the headmaster, but he had to work as a janitor to earn his room and board. When he finished his course in 1875, he returned to Malden where he taught school, took an active part in community life, and began a study of law in the informal fashion of the day. His was already a remarkable achievement.

In 1878 he went to Washington, D.C. and studied at Wayland Seminary. In childhood he had adopted

the surname of Washington. A year later he was called back to Hampton to speak at the commencement as a post-graduate and his performance apparently inspired the founder and director, General Samuel Chapman Armstrong, to invite him to join the faculty. After teaching the night class for a time, Washington became the prefect for a group of American Indian students whom Armstrong had succeeded in getting admitted to the school. His experience as supervisor honed the administrative skills that he would later require in order to fulfil the next stage in his career.

In 1881, General Armstrong received an appeal to send someone to Tuskegee, Alabama, to develop a school for Blacks on the Hampton model. A white person was specified, but Armstrong resolved to recommend Booker T. Washington. Arriving at Tuskegee, Washington discovered that he had to build it from the ground up.

The school actually held its first classes in a church while Washington, supported both morally and financially by friends at Hampton, moved rapidly to purchase a farm as the school site. Local fund-raising activities were devised and friends of Hampton were asked to send him money. Within a year, Tuskegee was on its way.

The first graduation ceremony at Tuskegee was held in 1885. By then Washington had recruited other teachers, mainly from Hampton, had established a firm local backing, and had interested Northern philanthropists in his undertaking. The Hampton connection was crucial to this early success, though Washington by the late 1880s had come to personal prominence through his careful pursuit of influential people and the power of his oratory.

Beginning in 1892, Washington convened an annual conference devoted to the problems of the Black farmer. This was simply one of the numerous activities he fostered and which made up the "Tuskegee Machine," a powerful network that was soon to have national, and even international, ramifications.

The grim underside of racism in the South – disfranchisement, violence, and economic exploitation – was viewed with distaste in the North. Accordingly, it welcomed the promise of a "New South" as first announced by Henry W. Grady, editor of the *Atlanta Constitution*, in an 1886 speech. He subsequently worked toward this goal in a variety of ways until his early death in 1889. Grady called for the industrialization of the South, aided by Northern capital, and believed that race relations would improve in the new economic climate he envisaged; he succeeded in winning over important segments of opinion, North and South.

The City of Atlanta, Georgia, where he lived, was profoundly marked by Grady's presence. In 1895 it held the Cotton States and International Exposition, exalting the vision of the New South, which drew some 800,000 visitors to a city of 75,000 people.

The year before, white Atlantans had sought a federal grant to help finance the planned exposition, and they had asked Booker T. Washington, now well-known as a Black educator, to appear with them before the congressional committee. They got their grant by a unanimous vote of the committee, perhaps because of the apparent biracial nature of the event. Later, when plans for a special

Facing page: Construction at the Tuskegee Institute at Tuskegee, Alabama, founded by Booker T. Washington in 1881.

Below: Booker T. Washington (seated left) and Emmett J. Scott (seated right), secretary of Tuskegee Institute and close associate of Washington, pose in front of the Institute with members of the staff.

building devoted to Black concerns were being considered, Washington was consulted. On the opening day of the exposition, September 18, 1895, Washington was one of the official speakers – after much backstage maneuvering. The speech he made has entered the annals of American history, and the exposition is now remembered mainly as the site of it.

Washington's speech, later called the "Atlanta Compromise" by Du Bois and others, was in fact a kind of amalgam of ideas he had expressed in earlier speeches, which had built up increasing support for his advocacy of industrial education for Blacks and of economic collaboration between Blacks and whites. The connection to Henry Grady was direct – Washington was well acquainted with his ideas and had corresponded with him. The great appeal of Washington's Atlanta speech, in the

Below: Prominent leaders of the Black Community in New York parade down Fifth Avenue with posters and banners pleading for equal rights.

Below: This statue of the mature Douglass by sculptor James E. Lewis is located on the campus of Morgan State University and was paid for, in part, by a subscription from the schoolchildren of Maryland.

climate of the exposition's self-congratulation, was its promise of peace, prosperity, and segregation. The speech ended with the words:

> In all things that are purely social we can be as separate as the fingers, yet one as the hand in all things essential to mutual progress.

Both the speech and the sentiment were approved by virtually all whites who heard or read it – and by most Blacks. It was this that propelled him to the leadership of his race in the United States.

A year after his Atlanta speech, Harvard University made Washington an honorary M.A. Back in Boston in 1900, he organized the National Negro Business League and in 1901 Dartmouth College conferred the LL.D. upon him. He was welcomed in the homes of the mighty, and his opinion and patronage were sought by Blacks and whites alike.

Booker T. Washington had become the most famous Southerner of his generation.

Douglass and the "Brave, Long Crusade"

The status of leader was conferred upon Washington because earlier in the year of the Atlanta speech, Frederick Douglass had died. At his death on February 20, 1895, he had been at the center of Black life in America for nearly 50 years, and for 34 of those years, he had been the most visible and eloquent representative of Black Americans in the country. He had experienced the yoke of slavery and the joy of escape, though with the constant fear of recapture. He had become known as orator, editor, and thinker in the

abolitionist cause. He had lived through the oppressive 1850s when the slaveholders demanded nothing less than absolute power – and went into a war of secession to get it. He had felt the exhilaration of the Civil War as a gateway to liberation, but also the despair of that war in the great cost of human life. He had held the highest hopes for Reconstruction, fired by an ambition for national unity and racial equality.

The Compromise of 1877 had been a sore burden to Douglass, although it did not diminish his faith in the Republican Party. In 1877 he had been honored with a patronage post as Marshal of the District of Columbia by President Hayes, over the objections of many whites. President Garfield, Hayes' successor, was urged to reappoint Douglass by Mark Twain, who wrote, "I offer this petition with peculiar pleasure and strong desire, because I so honor this man's high and blemishless character and so admire his brave, long crusade for the liberties and elevation of his race." Garfield did not make the reappointment, but he did give him the post of Recorder of Deeds.

In 1889 Douglass was appointed Minister to Haiti by President Harrison, a post he held for two years that were marked by controversy and vituperation from white Americans. He was highly esteemed by the Haitians, however, and the government of Haiti invited him to serve as commissioner for the Haitian pavilion at the World Colombian Exposition in Chicago in 1893. His speech at the dedication of the pavilion was a memorable one.

It is characteristic of Douglass that he kept an eye on the budding writers and artists of Black America. He knew the work of young Paul

Laurence Dunbar and Mary Church Terrell, for instance, and Mary Church Terrell remembered that Douglass read her the poem, *A Drowsy Day*, from a clipping from the *Indianapolis Journal* in the summer of 1892. At the Chicago Exposition, Douglass participated in a Colored American Day program, which featured poetry readings by Dunbar and singing by Harry T. Burleigh. Will Marion Cook, who was a violinist and composer, was the program organizer.

Douglass' last years were clouded by the horror of the lynchings in the South. He attacked this evil in solemn fury in a pamphlet published in 1894, ending it with this eloquent appeal:

> Put away your race prejudice.
> Banish the idea that one class
> must rule over another.
> Recognize the fact that the
> rights of the humblest citizens
> are as worthy of protection as
> are those of the highest and
> your problem will be solved,
> and – whatever may be in store
> for you in the future, whether
> prosperity or adversity,
> whether you have foes without
> or foes within, whether there
> shall be peace or war – based
> upon the eternal principles of
> truth, justice and humanity,
> with no class having cause for
> complaint or grievance, your
> Republic will stand and
> flourish forever.

The Du Bois Legacy

William Edward Burghardt Du Bois was born, like most Americans of his epoch, in a small town. His was Great Barrington, Massachusetts and the year was 1868. From this rural

hamlet nestling in the Berkshires, he was to come to world eminence, recognized variously as a historian, a sociologist, a civil rights leader, a peace movement leader, an editor, the father of Pan-Africanism, and ultimately as a shaper of both people and ideas.

In Du Bois' high school class of 13 students, only two or three planned to go to college. He aspired to go to Harvard but had to settle for Fisk University in Nashville, to which he won a scholarship. Although he was only 17, he was immediately placed in the sophomore class. Of this new stage in his life, Du Bois says:

> So I came to a region where the world was split into white and black halves, and where the darker half was held back by race prejudice and legal bonds, as well as by deep ignorance and dire poverty ... Into this world I leapt with enthusiasm. A new loyalty and allegiance replaced my Americanism: henceforward I was a Negro.

In a very real sense this was to be the meaning of Du Bois' life. The understanding and the vindication of the caste to which he was assigned in the United States – and its wider resonances – were to be the dominant theme in his long life. That life was one of unceasing activity until his death in Africa at the age of 95.

After graduation from Fisk, Du Bois achieved his ambition of study at Harvard when he was admitted as a junior at the age of 20. He then graduated *cum laude* two years later in a class of 300.

Du Bois remained at Harvard as a fellow for the next two years, study-

Previous pages, left: Elected a senator from Mississippi, Blanche K. Bruce served in a distinguished manner, working unsuccessfully for the equal application of the laws to Black and white alike.

Previous pages, right: One of the most outspoken foes of Booker T. Washington, William Monroe Trotter was frequently a "loner" in his crusade for equal rights. Like Du Bois, he had little patience with those whom he thought of as compromisers.

Left: W.E.B. Du Bois as a young man. He was to become a great shaper of both people and ideas.

ing history and political science. He earned his master's degree after one year of work and had virtually completed his doctoral dissertation in history at the end of the second year. That dissertation, *The Suppression of the African Slave Trade to the United States of America, 1638–1870*, was published in 1896, which was the same year he was awarded the doctorate.

Before that, from 1892 to 1894, Du Bois was in Europe, principally Germany. In his travels he savored the cultural delights of Vienna and Paris. But in June 1894 at the age of 26, he was home once more, ready to take up the challenge of serving his people. Wilberforce University in Ohio was the first school to offer him a job, as a teacher of the classics, and he accepted immediately. Later he received a telegram offering him a position teaching mathematics. It was from Booker T. Washington.

An interesting project fell his way the next year. The University of Pennsylvania had decided to undertake "The study of the social condition of the Colored People of the Seventh Ward of Philadelphia." Out of this study came Du Bois' *The Philadelphia Negro*, a monument of American sociology.

The Washington-Du Bois Controversy

The Washington-Du Bois controversy, variously interpreted, is a major motif in Afro-American history. Washington had come to national prominence as a result of his moderate Atlanta speech of 1895. Du Bois was among those who wrote to congratulate him. Du Bois later tells us:

I wrote to the *New York Age*

suggesting that there might be the basis of a real settlement between whites and blacks in the South, if the South opened to the Negroes the doors of economic opportunity and the Negroes cooperated with the white South in political sympathy. But this offer was frustrated by the fact that between 1895 and 1909 the whole South disfranchised its Negro voters . . .

Du Bois first came into conflict with Washington's ideas and influence in 1898. Washington had just been invited to join the Fisk Board of Trustees to help add industrial courses to the curriculum. The issue of industrial, as opposed to academic, education for young Blacks led to the first Du Bois attack on Washington, which took the form of a commencement address on Galileo. Washington, no matter what he might say, was perceived as condemning academic education for Blacks whereas Du Bois held that such education should at least be open to them. It was not very long before the controversy moved from education to politics. Washington's apparent acquiescence – at any rate, his public acquiescence – in the widespread disfranchisement of the Blacks in the South led Du Bois to stronger words of disagreement. His essay *Of Mr Booker T. Washington and Others*, lambasting Washington's stance, was the apex of *The Souls of Black Folk*, his landmark book of 1903. Its instant fame confirmed Du Bois as a leading challenger to the place of Booker T. Washington's authority in Black American life.

The NAACP

Du Bois called a group of Blacks together in June 1905 to explore strategies for improving the political and social fortunes of Black people. Twenty-nine of them gathered on the Canadian side of Niagara Falls to avoid the racial discrimination on the American side, and launched what became known as the Niagara Movement, whose principles were defined as:

1. Freedom of speech and criticism.
2. An unfettered and unsubsidized press.
3. Male suffrage.
4. The abolition of all caste distinctions based simply on race and color.
5. The recognition of the principle of human brotherhood.
6. The recognition of the highest and best human training as the monopoly of no class or race.
7. A belief in the dignity of labor.
8. United effort to realize these ideals under wise and courageous leaderships.

In the meantime a group of white Americans, horrified by lynchings and other anti-Black actions, called a conference in New York City in 1909. Du Bois and many members of the Niagara Movement accepted an invitation to participate in this conference and out of it came the National Association for the Advancement of Colored People (NAACP).

In 1910 Du Bois, who was a board member of the new organization, left his teaching post at Atlanta University to become the NACCP's Director of Publications and Research.

Below: W.E.B. Du Bois came to fame as the chief opponent of Booker T. Washington when he reproved the older man in *The Souls of Black Folk*. Prior to his activist period initiated by that book, Du Bois put his faith in scientific scholarship, represented by his historical study of the slave trade and his sociological study, *The Philadelphia Negro*.

His first project was to launch a magazine which was called *The Crisis* and which appeared in November 1910. He was to edit it until 1934.

The NAACP took as its task the enforcement of the Fourteenth and Fifteenth Amendments to assure Blacks the rights to education and the vote, the right to access in public places, and opposition to mob violence. The methods adopted from the start were legal challenges in the courts, and symbolic action intended to gain the public condemnation of injustice. Later this extended to the lobbying of state legislatures and congress.

From its inception in 1910 to the present, the NAACP has been at the center of the struggle for social justice for Black Americans. Over a long period of time, particularly in the area of employment and training, its efforts have been complemented by the National Urban League. In the Civil Rights era of the 1960s and 1970s, its work was supplemented and occasionally overshadowed by the Congress of Racial Equality (CORE), the Student Non-Violent Coordinating Committee (SNCC) and the Southern Christian Leadership Conference (SCLC), but over the years the NAACP has been without a doubt indispensable to the self-esteem of Black Americans.

Utopian Emigration

The oppressive conditions of life in the South, particularly in the rural South, made some Blacks dream of a home in a distant place as yet untouched by the bitter gall of racial prejudice. This image of an alternative life might be called utopian emigration, and it meant escape from near bondage, just as the Under-

Below: Although slavery had been abolished for several decades by the time this photograph was taken in the early 1900s, the cotton industry depended heavily on Black labor.

Above: The slaves of James Hopkinson of Edisto Island, South Carolina, posed for this early photograph in 1862.

ground Railroad had meant escape from real slavery in pre-Emancipation days. This time, the hope was to move families and communities in the expectation of long-term settlement or colonization.

Beginning in 1874, propaganda for migrating to Kansas, which had become a state in 1861, was circulated among Blacks in Tennessee and, later, in other hostile Southern states. One leader of this movement was Benjamin "Pap" Singleton, an ex-slave who had escaped to Canada and then returned to the United States following emancipation. Singleton called himself Moses and his followers Exodusters.

The Peak of the Exoduster movement was reached in 1897 when some 20,000 Blacks poured into Kansas. While many remained, the disappointment of many others was so deep that they returned home or went elsewhere.

Frederick Douglass, while recognizing the impulse of the Exodusters for a better life, deplored the movement and its implications for the future of Blacks in the South. In 1879 he addressed the American Social Science Association on the subject of the Exodus, using it to assess conditions then prevailing:

> Without abating one jot of our horror and indignation at the outrages committed in some parts of the Southern States against the Negro, we cannot but regard the present agitation of an African Exodus from the South as ill-timed, and in some respects hurtful. We stand today at the beginning of a grand and beneficent reaction. There is a growing recognition of the

Above: Benjamin "Pap" Singleton was one of the leaders of the Exoduster movement, which encouraged Blacks to migrate from the South to Kansas.

Facing page: This engraving from the *Illustrated Newspaper*, December 26, 1868 records the arrival of the first elected Black Congressman, John W. Menard of Louisiana, to the House of Representatives, although the House denied him his seat.

duty and obligation of the American people to guard, protect and defend the personal and political rights of all the people of the States; to uphold the principles upon which rebellion was suppressed, slavery abolished, and the country saved from dismemberment and ruin. We see and feel today, as we have not seen and felt before, that the time for conciliation, and trusting to the honor of the late rebels and slave-holders, has passed. The President of the United States himself, while still liberal, just and generous toward the South, has yet sounded a halt in that direction, and has bravely, firmly and ably asserted the constitutional authority, to maintain the public peace in every State, in the Union, and upon every day in the year; and has maintained this ground against all the powers of House and Senate.

Unfortunately Douglass' optimism about conditions and his faith in the Republican Party were unfounded, and compromised him in the eyes of many Blacks.

One Exoduster who did particularly well in Kansas was Edwin P. McCabe, later the chief figure in a Black move to the Oklahoma Territory in 1889. McCabe envisioned Oklahoma as a Black state with himself as governor, and helped found many all-Black towns in the territory. When Oklahoma became a state in 1907, however, it virtually disfranchised its Black population. A complete system of Jim Crow laws was enacted in a state that did not even have the excuse of Reconstruction for its actions.

Utopian emigration birthed a succession of African colonization efforts, beginning with the establishment in 1878 of the Liberian Exodus Joint Stock Steamship Company. This group actually obtained a ship and sent a small number of emigrants to Liberia in April of that year. This colonization effort should not be confused with the work of the American Colonization Society, which had been founded by whites in 1816 and was steadfastly opposed by most Black opinion down to the Civil War. The American Colonization Society had established Liberia as a homeland for free Blacks from the United States, but had in no way worked to obtain freedom for enslaved Blacks. This was seen as a moral flaw by most Blacks. Nevertheless, an important segment of Black opinion, hopelessly pessimistic about the American social order, came to consider colonization — under strictly Black auspices — as a possibility. One of those who swung toward emigration during the terrible 1850s, especially to Africa, was Martin Delaney and in 1859 he led a party to explore the Niger Valley for colonization purposes. In the 1870s, Delaney once more embraced the idea of emigration, lending his prestige as a former Union army soldier and Reconstruction political activist to the effort.

In 1894 the fiery AME bishop, Henry McNeal Turner, gave strong leadership to the African emigration movement by organizing the International Migration Society. The next year he took active part in the Congress on Africa held at the Gammon Theological Seminary in Atlanta, speaking on *The American Negro*

and the Fatherland. Under the sponsorship of the Society, 22 emigrants sailed to Liberia in 1895. The "African fever" of the 1890s, while not the last gasp of utopian emigration, closes the chapter on leaving the country as a goal in and of itself. Subsequent emigration programs arising in Black America have been related to religious movements.

The Black College

The American Missionary Association (AMA) was very important both for its own work and for the example it set in the founding of Black colleges. Its interest in Black progress was related to the fact that it grew in part out of the Amistad Committee. This group was formed to defend a group of Africans who in 1836 seized the Spanish slave vessel *Amistad* on which they were being shipped, killed or imprisoned the crew, and directed the pilots to sail back to Africa. By trickery the pilots sailed instead to the United States, where the ship was taken over by the Navy and all of the Africans arrested for mutiny. The Amistad Committee secured John Quincy Adams, former President of the United States, to defend the accused. They were finally freed in 1841, following a Supreme Court hearing of the case, and they returned home. The Amistad Committee later joined with other groups to form the American Missionary Association.

During and following the Civil War, the AMA sponsored or supported many educational endeavors among the freed slaves. Hampton Normal and Agricultural Institute (now Hampton University) and Atlanta University were two of their outstanding Black colleges.

Hampton Institute started as an

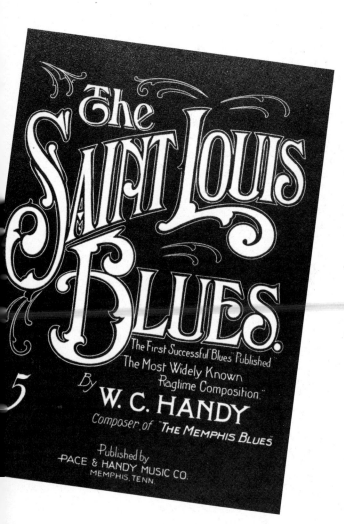

AMA school in 1861 in the Virginia city for which it was named – incidentally, the oldest continuously occupied English-speaking site in the Americas. In 1866 General Armstrong, then the Freedman Bureau's director of refugees in Eastern Virginia, persuaded the AMA to purchase a plantation containing a substantial stone manor house, which still stands – and here Hampton Institute was to develop. General Armstrong was the product of an educational and missionary tradition; he had studied at Williams College and was influenced by the example of his father, who had been superintendent of education in the Kingdom of Hawaii.

Hampton Institute was opened in 1868 on the principle of practical education, with a strong emphasis on industrial skills for men and home economics for women but with a broad and sound general education at the center of the school's program.

The school was run along military lines for men, although this approach was adapted for female students, and great emphasis was placed on promptness, hygiene, diligence, and responsibility. The two most distinguished students of Hampton in the nineteenth century, both of whom later served there as teachers and administrators, were Booker T. Washington, founder of Tuskegee Institute, and Robert R. Moton, Washington's successor. It is not surprising that Tuskegee was shaped in the Hampton image and constantly associated with it in the public mind.

Atlanta University owes its beginnings to the work of the Reverend Frederick Ayer and his wife, who came to Atlanta in 1865 and, in collaboration with Blacks already engaged in self-help, established the enterprise that was to become the University. It started in late 1866 as a school with Edmund Asa Ware, a young Yale graduate, as principal. In 1867 it was chartered as Atlanta University. Several of the early leaders of Atlanta University were Yale graduates and they developed the college program on the model of that excellent New England University.

Atlanta University graduated its first degree class in 1876, though there were preparatory and teacher training graduates before that. Among its most distinguished graduates are James Weldon Johnson, author, scholar, and diplomat; Walter White, author and civil rights pioneer; and Fletcher Henderson, composer, arranger, and originator of the big band tradition.

In 1929 Atlanta University became the graduate school in a consortium that included the two undergraduate schools of Morehouse College (for men) and Spelman College (for women). Both Morehouse and Spelman Colleges had been founded under the patronage of the American Baptist Home Mission Society. Later the consortium was extended to take in Clark College and Morris Brown College.

W.E.B. Du Bois taught at the University from 1897 to 1910, when it was an undergraduate school, and returned as a professor in the graduate school, from 1933 to 1944. Several of his most important works were written while he was there, including *The Souls of Black Folk*, *John Brown* and *Black Folk – Then and Now*.

Blues, Ragtime, Jazz

It is safe to say that the spiritual, a product of the Folk-Rural Culture, virtually ceased to be created after Emancipation – although it con-

tinued to be performed. In fact, the publication of *Slave Songs of the United States* in 1867 came at the moment when the music it introduced to the larger world was destined to decline.

The blues were the new vocal music of Black America. In contrast to the spiritual, the blues are in no sense a community product, but are rather an individual creation directed to an audience. With the coming of the blues also comes the performing artist for the blues are the work of performers who have consciously developed artistic skills, for an audience which is prepared to listen – and sometimes to pay for hearing it.

It is not possible to trace the blues to their source but worksongs, Black narrative songs or ballads, and the spiritual all made some contribution. *The Memphis Blues* of 1912 was the first piece published as blues. It was probably arranged rather than composed by W.C. Handy, later called the Father of the Blues. Handy was a well-trained bandmaster with wide-ranging musical interests – in 1914 he published *The Saint Louis Blues*, memorably recorded in 1925 by Bessie Smith with Louis Armstrong on cornet. The blues form and sentiment are typified in these stanzas of Bessie Smith's own *Lost Your Head Blues*, recorded in 1926:

I was with you baby, when you
didn't have a dime
I was with you baby, when you
didn't have a dime
Now that you got plenty money,
you have throwed your good girl
down
When you were lonesome, I tried to
treat you kind
When you were lonesome, I tried to
treat you kind

Facing page: Gertrude "Ma" Rainey was widely known as the Queen of the Blues.

Below: Scott Joplin was the greatest of the composers of piano ragtime. He had high and serious ambitions, which reached fruition in his opera *Treemonisha*, first given a professional performance long after his death at Symphony Hall in Atlanta.

But since you got money, it's done
changed your mind
Days are lonesome, nights are long
Days are lonesome, nights are so
long
I'm a good girl, but I've been
treated wrong

Blues have been classified as rural or country and urban or city. Rural blues may represent an earlier stage, but the two traditions coexist and intertwine. Rural blues are usually performed by singers who accompany themselves on guitar, and well-known exponents include Papa Charlie Jackson, who made the first recording of a country blues in 1924, Blind Lemon Jefferson, and Huddie Ledbetter. Ledbetter, more commonly called Leadbelly, also composed other kinds of music.

Urban blues, sometimes also called classic blues, are typically performed by a singer backed by an instrumental group. While Mamie Smith was the first singer to record a classic blues in 1920, the most famous blues singers are Gertrude "Ma" Rainey and Bessie Smith, both of whom toured extensively, particularly in the South, during the 1920s. In a general way, rural blues have been associated with male singers and urban blues with female singers. Louis Armstrong is a notable example of the few men who have performed urban blues, often alternating as instrumentalists.

Just as the blues are a bridge between the Folk-Rural and Folk-Urban Black Cultures, ragtime music forms a bridge between the Folk-Urban and the general American culture in the period from the 1890s to World War I. In essence, ragtime is piano music with strong syncopation, based on Black percussive and banjo styles. Methods of "ragging" existing tunes were practised by many Black piano performers in the 1890s and Blacks remained the dominant innovators and players of ragtime, though their techniques were quickly adapted by white performers. The first original ragtime music published by a Black composer was Tom Turpin's *Harlem Rag* in 1897. Turpin, who ran a saloon in St Louis, later published *St Louis Rag* (1903) and *Buffalo Rag* (1904), his last. In 1899 Scott Joplin came on the scene with *The Maple Leaf Rag*. The popularity of this piece and a succession of others from his hands made him widely recognized as the leading exponent of this type of music. Other important ragtime composers are James Scott and James F. Lamb, a white composer. The Joplin tradition is often referred to as classic ragtime.

Ragtime, fundamentally piano music, was adapted for instrumental groups and entered the theatres and dancehalls that were favorite haunts of Americans at the turn of the twentieth century.

Jazz, like ragtime, is rooted in the 1890s Folk-Urban Culture, but its origins lie in the band tradition, which was nourished by the blues and ragtime. The band tradition as a pre-jazz element was to be found throughout Folk-Urban America by the turn of the century, from New York to St Louis, from Chicago to Mobile, from Kansas City to Baltimore, and from Washington to Charleston.

But the birthplace of jazz is undoubtedly New Orleans. A variety of circumstances had endowed New Orleans with a richness of musical resources and traditions. There was its tradition of orchestras whose

Below: Scott Joplin was king in the realm of classic ragtime.

Facing page: A virtuoso on clarinet and soprano saxophone, Sidney Bechet spent a large part of his career in France, where he became a major point of contact between American jazz and European patrons and performers of this music.

members were Creoles of color descended from free people – these seated ensembles played concert and dance music, and there were also the marching bands, like military ones. These were popular with the city's black working class, an amalgam of the older urban slave population and latecomers from the rural areas. The two band traditions of New Orleans, involving literally hundreds of players, took enrichment from the blues and ragtime and the result was jazz: vocals wedded to instrumental music, rhythmic, improvisational, but grounded in solid musical craft and technique.

Dozens of performers and creators are associated with early jazz, which does not enter recording history until 1917. The first record was of a white group from New Orleans, the Original Dixieland Jazz Band, performing the *Darktown Strutters Ball*. Oral history points to Charles "Buddy" Bolden as a central figure in the creation of jazz in New Orleans in the mid-1890s. Joseph "King" Oliver, a virtuoso on the cornet, was another leading figure. His was the first major jazz group to record extensively, beginning in 1923. Edward "Kid" Ory, King Oliver's contemporary and the first great jazz trombonist, made some recordings in 1922. Louis Armstrong, considered by many to be the greatest jazz musician of them all, played cornet with both King Oliver and Kid Ory, and later recorded with his own back-up groups. Another New Orleans musician of note was Sidney Bechet, a marvel on the soprano saxophone and the clarinet.

Jazz originally had no listening audience, being meant as dance or marching music – the passive audience came when non-Blacks became interested in it. From the first, jazz musicians were highly conscious of each other's performance and, in some degree, played for themselves. The jam session, when musicians gather together to play their best performance possible both for and with each other, is a tradition arising from this aspect of jazz performance.

Jam sessions are truly unrehearsed, the music improvised out of the creative energy released by friendly competition. Throughout jazz history, the jam session has

DEDICATED TO JAMES BROWN AND HIS MANDOLIN CLUB

THE ENTERTAINER

BY SCOTT JOPLIN

COMPOSER OF

MAPLE LEAF RAG
SUNFLOWER SLOW DRAG
PEACHERINE RAG
SWIPESY CAKE WALK
THE STRENUOUS LIFE (RAG)
THE RAGTIME DANCE (SONG)
ETC., ETC.

A RAG TIME TWO STEP

50

JOHN STARK & SON
SHEET MUSIC PUBLISHERS
ST. LOUIS

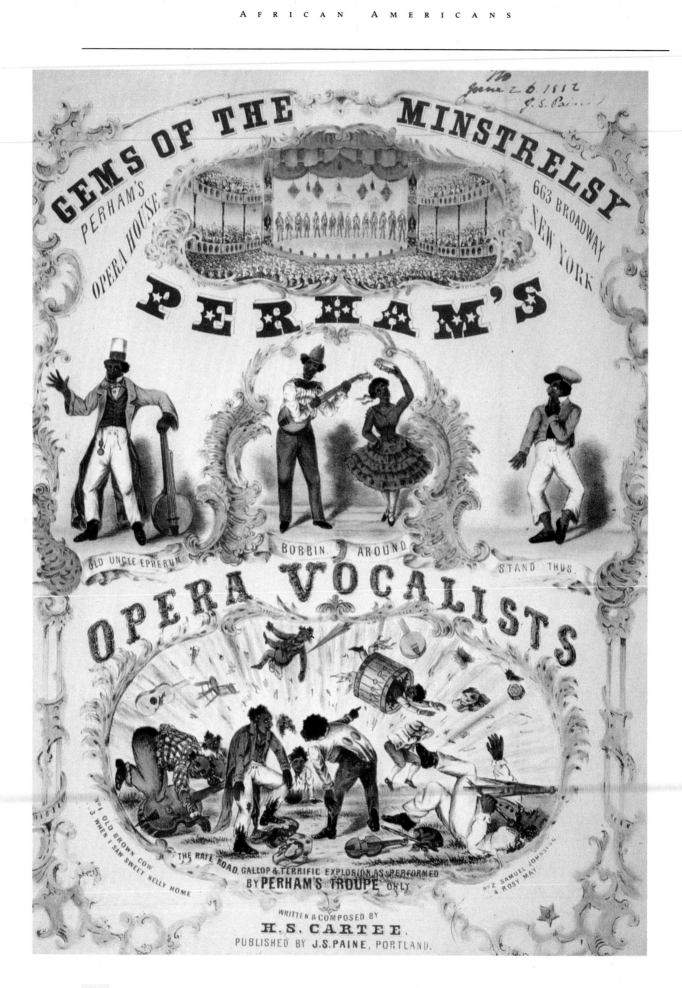

spawned the innovations and advances in technique that make it unique, especially in its period of growth from the 1890s to post-World War II. Public performances of jazz are far less improvisational, though the best may have impromptu passages and always sound spontaneous.

The Minstrel Show

The black-faced minstrel show was a paradoxical form of entertainment that developed in the United States before the Civil War. In it, white male performers gave comic imitations of Blacks. The minstrel show included comedy acts and funny songs, dances, and sentimental songs. The most famous composer of minstrel show songs was Stephen Foster, whose *Old Folks at Home* and *Camptown Races* are typical.

The first famous troupe was Dan Emmett's Virginia Minstrels, but it was Edwin P. Christy who set the minstrel format. His troupe toured widely both in the United States and England, and he had many imitators. The standard show, which had become set by 1860, consisted of three parts. Part one presented the whole cast, faces blackened, seated in a semicircle. In the center sat the "interlocutor", who was the master of ceremonies, and on each end sat the chief comics, Mr Tambo and Mr Bones, who held a musical instrument associated with his name. They were called the end men. Humor, including riddles and puns, was interwoven with sentimental songs and dances in this first part of the program, which ended with the "walk-around."

The second part of the show was the olio. It was more of a mixture, with various specialty acts holding the stage in succession, and there was usually some mock preaching called "stump speaking." The third part was a play, generally either a sentimental portrayal of happy plantation life or a comical parody or burlesque.

It seems bizarre that, with Blacks and slavery at the center of the nation's concern in the decades before the Civil War, minstrels should become the most popular entertainment. Many reasons have been put forward for it, including that the ridiculous and farcical presentation of Blacks, making them grotesque characters, served to exorcise the feelings of guilt raised by abolitionists among whites in the North, where the minstrels flourished.

After the Civil War, the minstrel show was changed. It tended toward more elaborate entertainment, the addition of brass bands, and the introduction of female characters. The most important new note was the development of Black minstrel companies, bringing to the stage talented Black performers, some of

Facing page: This poster is a typical example of the advertising used to advise the public of the arrival of a minstrel group in town.

Below: A Negro band in New Orleans, 1910. Brass bands had an influence in early jazz and blues.

whom had been slaves. The Black Minstrel troupes thrived until the 1890s and were the training ground for all types of Black performers during this period.

While taking up the format already developed by white companies, with which they were now in competition, the Black performers lessened the intensity and frequent viciousness of the caricatures. Except for Mr Tambo and Mr Bones, Black performers whitened their faces – and the whole paradox came full circle.

One of the most influential Black minstrels was Charles Hicks. After organizing troupes in the late 1860s, he toured Europe for a few years and later took a company to Australia for three years. Hicks was both a versatile performer and a clever publicist and manager. In his own country, however, he was barred from success by white managers who controled the theatres and entertainment circuits.

The leading post-Civil War song writer was the Black composer James Bland, whose *Carry Me Back to Ole Virginny* and *Oh, Dem Golden Slip-*

pers have won enduring popularity. Bland was also a minstrel performer, a singer and an elegant comic. Having gone to England with the Haverly Colored Minstrels, he remained in Europe for several years performing in music halls there.

Black Musicals

Musical entertainment in the theater was changing in America – it was moving from a variety format to a show based on a libretto or book. Under the influence of this change, the Black minstrel show evolved into the Black musical, a new kind of stage show which opened up more opportunities for female performers, who had been blocked by the minstrel tradition of all-male casts.

As early as 1891 *The Creole Show* opened in Boston with an all-Black cast, but this was more a revue than a musical with a book. Its main importance is that it was put on at the Chicago World's Fair in 1893 and served to introduce a large audience to Black musical talent. In April 1898 the Black musical *A Trip to Coontown* was presented at a somewhat obscure New York theater. Created by Bob Cole and Billy Johnson, it met with an unenthusiastic response. The following summer, however, the short musical called *Clorindy or The Origin of the Cakewalk* caused a

Left: Called "Black Patti" in emulation of the great operatic singer, Adeline Patti, Sissieretta Jones organized and toured with troupes of talented performers, including actors, comedians, and musicians. The high point of her shows was always her own performance of sentimental and Euro-classical music.

Below: Another poster advertising the arrival of a minstrel group.

Facing page: The Edward LeRoy Rice Minstrel troup performing at the White House. Note that the performers are in fact white men in Black faces.

SOMETHING TO PLEASE EVERYBODY
IS EVER A WATCHWORD WITH THE MANAGEMENT OF

BAIRD'S MAMMOTH MINSTRELS

Which is now Absolutely The Strongest Show! The Greatest Show! The Best Show before the People of America To-Day.

THE BEST
PLENTY OF
THE BEST
AND
NOTHING BUT
THE BEST
IS THE
SECRET
OF OUR
SUBLIME
SUCCESS.

A
HOST
OF
HAPPY
SURPRISES
A BLOOMING
GARDEN
OF
RARE
NOVELTIES.

PROMINENT IN THE ATTRACTIVE PROGRAM IS

THE GRAND IDEAL CLOG BALLET "AMERICA"

Below: Bert Williams, George Walker and his wife Aida Overton Walker appear on stage together. Williams was an actor and comedian of great subtlety. The earliest part of his career was bound up with George Walker, who was also a singer, dancer, and inspired comic.

Far right: Aida Overton Walker was a graceful and talented ingenue who made a memorable impact on theater goers for many years, starting with her appearance in the operetta In Dahomey. Later she assumed a dancing part, which was created by her husband, George Walker, when he fell ill.

Right: An actress and a singer in the classical tradition, Abbie Mitchell appeared frequently on Broadway and in recital. She was in the original production of Gershwin's opera, Porgy and Bess.

sensation. It had a book by Paul Laurence Dunbar and music by Will Marion Cook, and starred Ernest Hogan of minstrel fame. The same summer, Cole and Johnson opened their *Kings of Koon-dom*, which clearly owed its origins to the tradition of the minstrel.

The first full Black musical to play on Broadway was *In Dahomey*, which opened in February 1903. White critics thought it equal to other full Broadway shows, they did not find it necessarily outstanding. Produced by Bert Williams and George Walker, *In Dahomey* had a score by Cook and lyrics by Dunbar.

The comic talent of Bert Williams brought grudging admission that he might be America's funniest comedian. The slim libretto by J.A. Shipp concerns a fraudulent colonization scheme. The cakewalk scenes and the African-style dancing raised the Broadway temperature and, all in all, the show clearly possessed a high level of artistry in music and dance.

In spite of its merits, *In Dahomey* had a relatively short Broadway run because of general prejudice and specific maneuvering by white Broadway. Subsequently the show went to London where it was wildly applauded and ran for seven months.

Williams and Walker next produced *In Abyssinia* in 1906. Once more the score was by Cook and the libretto by J.A. Shipp. It, too, had a short run.

A white producer, Ray Comstock, assembled the same team to create *Bandana Land* in 1907. Its commercial success was somewhat greater than *In Abyssinia*, though it recycled the now hardened formula of Black musicals: dialect songs and the cakewalk at the climax. Later the same year, Williams and Walker returned as the star and producer of *The Shoo-Fly Regiment*. This was the last venture of this Broadway partnership, although Bert Williams went on to work either alone or with other partners.

The brothers James Weldon Johnson, lyricist, and J. Rosamond Johnson, composer, had had a hand in the unfortunate *A Trip to Coontown* of 1898. Two years later they contributed songs to a white show, *The Belle of Bridgeport*, starring May Irwin. In 1904, working with Bob Cole, they contributed songs to another white musical, *In Newport*.

Cole and J. Rosamond Johnson were associated with other shows, writing lyrics and songs as well as performing. In one of these, *The Red Moon* of 1909, the lead was the singer Abbie Mitchell, wife of Will Marion Cook. James Reese Europe was the orchestra conductor. Blacks lost what little ground they had gained on Broadway in the decade immediately following 1910.

Paul Laurence Dunbar

The most noteworthy poet in the United States in the decade 1895–1905 was the tragic Paul Laurence Dunbar. No other American poetry written in that period has endured.

Dunbar was born in 1872 in Dayton, Ohio, to parents who had been slaves and who had become part of the great internal migration that created the Folk-Urban Culture on which the poet was to be a major influence. At 21, when Dunbar was working as an elevator operator for lack of other opportunities, he published his first volume of poetry at his own expense. Called *Oak and Ivy*, it appeared in 1893. His next book, *Majors and Minors* (1895), brought him national attention following a review by William Dean Howells. In 1896 came *Lyrics of Lowly Life*, with an introduction by Howells, and Dunbar's fame was assured. Later volumes were *Lyrics of the Hearth-side* (1879), *Lyrics of Love and Laughter* (1903), and *Lyrics of Sun-shine and Shadow* (1905). Before his early death in 1906, Dunbar had also published four novels and four volumes of short stories. He had a lively interet in the theater and wrote several works for the stage in colla-boration with the composer Will Marion Cook. His other musical col-laborators were Samuel Coleridge-Taylor and Harry T. Burleigh.

Dunbar has a special place in the history of Black American culture because of his hold on the public imagination. From the mid-1890s until fairly recent times, his poems — especially some of those in dialect — enjoyed extraordinary popularity with amateur performers. Many hundreds of people in Black communities gained local celebrity because of the recitation of Dunbar poems on the "concert party" circuit, at churches, Sunday teas, lodge meetings, and socials of all description.

In 1920 Alice Dunbar-Nelson, his wife, published *The Dunbar Speaker and Entertainer* containing a selection of his most popular platform pieces. But long before, many of these has been the property of many reciters and elocutionists.

Among the most popular of Dunbar's genre works is the dramatic *In the Morning*, which opens with these stanzas:

'Lias! 'Lias! Bless de Lawd!
Don' you know de day's erbroad?
Ef you don't git up, you scamp,
Dey'll be trouble in dis camp.
T'ink I gwine to let you sleep
W'ile I meks yo' boa'd an' keep?
Dat's a putty howdy-do-
Don' you hyeah me, 'Lias – you?

Bet ef I come crost dis flo'
You won' fin' no time to sno'.
Daylight all a-shinin' in
W'ile you sleep – w'h hit's a sin!
Ain't de can'le-light enough
To bu'n out widout a snuff,
But you go de m'nin' thoo
Bu'nin' up de daylight too?

'Lias, don' you hyeah me call?
No use tu'nin' to'ds de wall;
I kin hyeah dat mattuss squeak?
Don' you hyeah me w'en I speak?
Dis hyeah clock done struck off six
Ca'line, bring me dem ah sticks!
Oh, you down, suh; huh, you down –
Look hyeah, don' you daih to frown.

Dunbar had mixed feelings about the greater popularity of his dialect poems over his others. He gave expression to this in *The Poet:*

Facing page: During his brief period of literary activity, Paul Laurence Dunbar was one of the best-known and most popular poets in the United States. For the first half of the twentieth cen-tury, he was quoted and "performed" for Afro-American audi-ences to an extent exceeded only by the King James version of the Bible.

He sang of life, serenely sweet,
With, now and then, a deeper note.
From some high peak, nigh yet
remote.
He voiced the world's absorbing
beat.
He sang of love when earth was
young,
And Love itself, was in his lays.
But ah, the world, it turned to
praise
A jingle in a broken tongue.

He was too hard on himself, for his dialect poems were neither "jingles" nor "in a broken tongue." Rather they were the medium in which his comic genius and sensitivity to pathos flowered. His achievement in the medium won the high opinion of his contemporaries and the esteem of later generations. In the 1970s, for example, the choreographer Louis Johnson created a very witty ballet suggested by *While Malindy Sings.*

Oh, hit's sweetah dan de music
Of an edicated band;
An' hit's dearah dan de battle's
Song o'triumph in de lan'.
It seems holier dan evenin'
When de solemn chu'ch bell rings,
Ez I sit an' ca'mly listen
While Malindy sings.

Scholarly Activists

It was virtually unthinkable for any Black Americans who had gained an education not to work actively for the advancement of their people. An important book by William J. Simmons, *Men of Mark: Eminent, Progressive, and Rising* (1887), provides sketches of over 150 scholarly activists. These include W.S. Scarborough, John Mercer Langston, Alexander Crummell, E.M. Brawley, and Bishop Benjamin

Tucker Tanner. These last two were both fathers of very distinguished children – Benjamin Brawley, historian and literary critic, and Henry O. Tanner, painter,

George Washington Williams and William H. Sheppard, both of whom became directly involved in African questions, Kelly Miller, and Carter G. Woodson, are all typical of this tradition.

George Washington Williams was born in 1849 in Pennsylvania. As a teenager he enlisted in the Union army and after demobilization he served in the Mexican army. Returning from his youthful military service, he entered the Newton Theological Seminary and completed his studies in 1874. He was ordained in the Baptist church, though his father had been a Unitarian and his mother a Lutheran. Taking pulpits first in Boston and Washington, D.C., he went to Cincinnati in 1876. Not long after, he resigned from the church to accept an appointment in the government service. Concurrently he studied law and was admitted to the bar in 1881.

Williams was a highly disciplined man of encyclopedic interests and vast talents. He wrote two histories that fully met the scholarship standards of the period, *A History of the Negro Race in America from 1619 to 1880* (1883) and *A History of the Negro Troops in the War of Rebellion* (1888). The first was not equalled in scope until Woodson's *The Negro in Our History* and the second not until Benjamin Quarles' *The Negro in the Civil War.*

Williams took a lively interest in the European powers' "scramble for Africa" and in the Berlin Conference of 1884. He was the author of an unsolicited and disregarded *Report*

Facing page: Called by some the "director" of the Washington DC branch of the Harlem Renaissance, Georgia Douglas Johnson was a poet who pursued traditional themes.

Above: Scholar George W. Williams was a man of encyclopedic interests and vast talent.

Right: Black inventor Lewis Latimar executed the patent drawings for the telephone in 1876, invented the carbon filament electric lamp in 1881, and installed some of the first electric street lights in New York City in 1882.

upon the Congo State and Country to the President of the Republic of the U.S. (1886). In 1890 he addressed an open letter to King Leopold of Belgium about Congo affairs. Other ambitious projects were cut short by his death in 1891.

William H. Sheppard was born in 1865 in Virginia. At 15 he went to Hampton Institute and later to Tuscaloosa Institute (now Stillman College). Ordained in the Presbyterian church, he wanted more than anything to go to Africa as a missionary but the white leadership of the Southern Presbyterian church was at first reluctant to engage a Black missionary, even to go to Africa, although they eventually relented. Sheppard went with a white colleague who died just a year after they had established the American Presbyterian Congo Mission in April 1891.

Sheppard's enthusiasm for Africa led him to learn local languages and to make a systematic study of the life around him. He developed a great interest in the Kuba visitors to the town in which the mission was established and decided to extend his mission to their kingdom. They, however, did not want Westerners in their territory and threatened all foreigners with execution, but Sheppard managed to penetrate Kuba land in 1892. He and his party were taken prisoner on the order of the king, but he caused much confusion by speaking their language fluently. In the end, he was allowed to establish a residence in the capital and stayed for four months under orders not to leave without permission. When he eventually received permission to go, he left two of his African attendants as hostages.

Sheppard's observations and reports on the Kuba made him a cel-

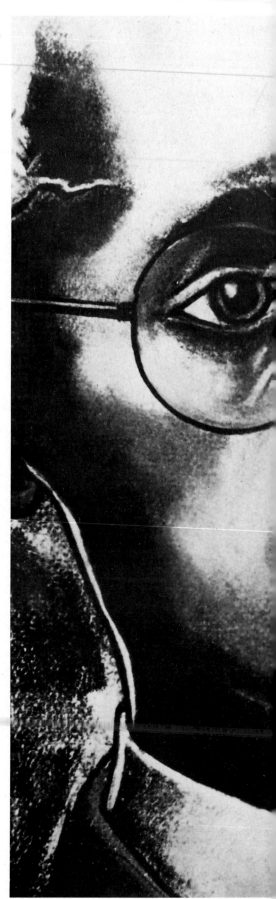

ebrity. He lectured on them at Hampton Institute and published articles in the *Southern Workman*, which was printed there. Nearly 20 years later, Hampton purchased the bulk of Sheppard's collection of Kuba art objects, and these are still in the University Museum there.

Sheppard paid one return visit to the Kuba. He continued his missionary work until 1910, but ran into difficulties because of his outspoken opposition to the colonial policies of Belgian companies in the Congo. when he was sued for libel by the Compagnie du Kasai, he was vindicated in the courts. Sheppard, who was elected a fellow of the Royal geographical Society, died in 1927. The library at Stillman College is named in his honor.

Kelly Miller, born in South Carolina in 1863, studied at Howard University and later at Johns Hopkins University, which subsequently refused Black students for many decades. He returned to Howard University in Washington, D.C., first as a teacher of mathematics and then of sociology. Miller became a national figure on the strength of his oratorical and analytical skills, which he used to advance his people.

In the period when the Washington-Du Bois controversy was a major concern of articulate Black Americans, Miller attempted to adopt a middle path. With time he came more and more to reject Washington's position, which too easily lent itself to conservative and reactionary interpretation. His earlier views are collected in *Race Adjustment* (1908). A later collection, *Out of the House of Bondage* (1914), is less middle-of-the road. In 1919 he published *History of the World War and the Important Part Taken by Negroes* as a propaganda statement for the advancement of Blacks.

His most famous political writing is *An Open Letter to Thomas Dixon, Jr.*, an attack on Dixon's rabid racism. Dixon had much to answer for as the author of a number of anti-Black works. His novel, *The Leopard's Spots*, was the basis for D.W. Griffith's landmark film, *The Birth of A Nation*, which is criticized today for its white supremacist bias.

Carter G. Woodson was a Virginian, born in 1875, who worked as a coal miner before he was able to go to high school. Then he attended Berea College and the University of Chicago, where he ultimately gained a Ph.D., in history from Harvard. He taught in the Philippines following the Spanish-American War and the U.S. occupation of the former Spanish colony.

Woodson worked briefly at West Virginia State College and Howard University, but his consuming passion was to establish Black history studies on a sound basis. To that end, he founded the Association for the Study of Negro Life and History in Washington in 1915. The following year he began publication of a quarterly called *The Journal of Negro History*. He also published several scholarly books through his own firm, the Associated Publishers.

Woodson wrote a succession of works, including *The Education of the Negro Prior to 1861* (1915), *A Century of Negro Migration* (1918), and *The History of the Negro Church* (1927). He made his greatest impact with *The Negro in Our History*, a textbook based mostly on original research. The book went through many editions and after Woodson's death in 1950, it was revised by Charles Wesley.

Above: This portrait
of W.E.B. Du Bois
by Frederick J.
Campbell is in the
collection of Atlanta
University.

CHAPTER III

BLACK AMERICA
EMERGES

Below: The imperious Bessie Smith, quintessential blues singer.

The entrance of the United States into the 1914–1918 European war, known at the time as the Great War because of its scale and ferocity, was momentous for Black America. The labor demands created by wartime production in the industrial North sparked a massive South-to-North migration, and this brought about a fundamental change in Black American life. It resulted in what may be called the Trans-Urban Culture.

The migration that had led to the development of the Folk-Urban Culture had been chiefly to cities of the South and the Border states. The World War I movement was not only bigger in scale but also drew Blacks from both the urban and rural South to the urban North. For a number of reasons, Blacks settled in certain sections of the cities of the North, later to be called ghettos. Before that derogatory word came to be used, Blacks felt a certain exhilaration in the idea of constituting a city within a city, freed of the restrictive Jim Crow laws of the South.

Trans-Urban Culture is the result of the linking up of the new urban concentrations of Blacks across the country, South and North, East and West. The linkages were due largely to the ease of travel from city to city by rail, and in part to the developing technologies that were transforming the whole United States: the phonograph, motion pictures, and radio. For example, records brought Bessie Smith and other Black entertainers into the homes of countless Blacks throughout America's cities. It is interesting to notice, too, how many blues songs allude to train travel, and how much jazz sonorities and rhythms reflect the sound of the steam locomotive.

The Black Press

The first Black Abolitionist newspaper was James Russwurm's *Freedom's Journal*, but it was overshadowed by Frederick Douglass' *The North Star*, which was known to virtually every literate Black person living in the cities of the North during the 1850s. In the late nineteenth and early twentieth centuries, there were a number of small Black newspapers that had limited local circulation.

T. Thomas Fortune founded the

New York Globe (later *The New York Age*) in 1879 and later worked for other newspapers as editor and correspondent. He was a crusading editor who took issue with Frederick Douglass on Black support of the Republican Party. Fortune wrote *Black and White: Land, Labor, and Politics in the South* (1884) and *The Negro in Politics* (1885). In 1887 he formed a protest organization, the Afro-American League. Lack of sustained support led him to accept secret help from Booker T. Washington, an arrangement that seems to have demoralized him.

Ida Wells Barnett established her reputation on a crusade against lynching. She lectured widely and wrote the pamphlet *The Red Record* to carry her campaign beyond the newspapers. Her autobiography was edited and published many years after her death by her daughter Alfreda Duster.

William Monroe Trotter, who had been a classmate of W.E.B. Du Bois at Harvard, edited the *Boston Guardian.* He attacked the Booker T. Washington policy of racial accommodation not only in print, but also by direct action. Like Fortune, he established an organization to carry out the political goals he promoted, the National Rights League, and he later joined with Du Bois in organizing the Niagara Movement.

The pattern for the function of the Black Press in the Trans-Urban era was set by the *Chicago Defender,* founded in the Black Belt of Chicago by Robert S. Abbott, a native of Georgia. His newspaper became truly national, gaining countrywide circulation through broad-based networks. The *Defender* played a leading role in encouraging Blacks to migrate from the South during World War I, which caused it to be banned in many Southern communities, although it continued to circulate surreptitiously. Other newspapers that became national by the 1920s were the *Pittsburgh Courier* founded by Robert L. Vann, *The Baltimore Afro-American* published by the Murphy family, and the *Norfolk Journal and Guide* established by P.B. Young.

The setting up of the Associated Negro Press by Claude A. Barnett in Chicago provided a press service for hundreds of smaller local newspapers, bringing them into the Trans-Urban network staked out by the larger papers. Some of the big cities offered a choice of several Black newspapers in the period from 1920 to 1940. Black Philadelphians, for example, could read the local *Philadelphia Tribune* and *Philadelphia Independent*, as well as the Philadelphia editions of the *Afro-American* and *Courier.*

Two other publications that played an important role along with the newspapers, were *Crisis,* founded by Du Bois as the organ of the NAACP, and *Opportunity,* the voice of the Urban League, which was founded in 1923 and edited by Charles S. Johnson.

A feeling of hope had been induced in Black migrants by the prospect of higher wages in the factories of the North. Unfortunately, this was almost immediately offset by profiteering landlords who charged steep rents for overcrowded lodgings. Other disillusionments dogged them, too. A certain sense of euphoria had been created by the World War I motto, "Make the world safe for democracy." That democracy could exclude Blacks was made clear by continued discrimination when

Black veterans returned from the war, and a series of Northern race riots expressed Black discontent with this state of affairs. Nevertheless, the general mood of Blacks in the decade of the twenties – the start of the Trans-Urban Culture – was upbeat.

The New Negro

The New Negro (1925), an anthology of poetry, fiction, and critical and historical essays, was compiled and edited by Alain Locke, Professor of Philosophy at Howard University. Based on a special Harlem issue of the influential intellectual magazine *Survey Graphic*, which appeared in March 1925, it had an incredible success among Blacks and whites interested in what they perceived as a unique flowering of Black creativity.

The New Negro remains a document unique in kind and permanent in value. It became the voice of a movement, carrying the Harlem Renaissance far beyond the borders of the United States, and it lies behind the Negritude movement of France and the Caribbean. It was a personal inspiration to most subsequent Black American writers.

The New Negro and the Garvey Movement

A newspaper publishing articles in three languages was *The Negro World*, the organ of the Universal Negro Improvement Association (UNIA), founded by Marcus M. Garvey. Marcus Garvey had emigrated from Jamaica in 1916 and by 1920 created an organization large enough and important enough to attract nationwide attention. The Garvey Movement, so rapid in its growth, is one of the most striking phenomena of the Trans-Urban Culture. Based in New York City, the

UNIA had branches in most cities with Black communities although there were fewer in the urban South and none at all in the rural South.

It was Garvey who first popularized the term "New Negro" in his many speeches, though William Pickens had published a book of that title in 1916. Garvey was one of the greatest orators of his generation. His message was one of race pride and economic self-sufficiency and his vision was "Africa for the Africans," a home for all of the descendants of Black Africa abroad. In a symbolic convention held in New York City in 1920, Garvey had himself declared "Provisional President of Africa" and appointed a cabinet.

Though the UNIA organized a shipping company and other enterprises, and though it founded the African Orthodox Church, the movement gravitated around the person and personality of Garvey himself. So, when Garvey got into trouble with the Federal government in 1923 because of the implication of his movement for political and social change, the movement began to weaken. More trouble led to his imprisonment in 1925 and his deportation in 1927, and after that, the movement quickly fell apart.

Pan-Africanism

In July 1900, W.E.B. Du Bois participated in a Pan-African Conference called in London by the Trinidadian lawyer, Henry Sylvester Williams. Du Bois was named Secretary of the conference and drafted its resolutions. In the *Report* of the conference he first gave utterance to the words, "The problem of the twentieth century is the problem of the color line."

The loss of Germany's African colonies to the allies at the end of World War I was the beginning of a long-lived attempt by Du Bois to get these colonies under international trusteeship, to prepare them for self-government. As soon as was practicable after the war, Du Bois called what has since become known as the First Pan-African Congress, which took place in Paris in February 1919, while the Versailles Conference was still sitting.

Three other Pan-African Congresses followed. Du Bois described the second one, in 1921, as "a large and influential meeting with delegates from the whole Negro World. The wide publicity it gained led to the organization of congresses in many parts of Africa by the natives." However, the attempt to form a permanent secretariat in Paris failed. The third congress, this time a much smaller one, was held in London and Lisbon in 1923; and in 1927 a disappointing fourth congress was held in New York.

Du Bois resisted appeals to call another congress in the 1930s and it was not until the end of World War II that one was convened, in Manchester, England in October 1945. It was propelled by George Padmore as Secretary and supported by Kwame Nkrumah and Jomo Kenyatta; Du Bois, now the elder statesman of Pan-Africanism, was elected International President, presiding over a phalanx of Africans who would lead their nations to the political independence he had always dreamed of and worked for. Du Bois seems to have been the only Afro-American present, a sign perhaps of Black America's determination to better their conditions at home.

At this fifth Pan-African Congress, Du Bois became more aware of the demands for independence by

Previous pages: The themes of the Universal Negro Improvement Association, which Marcus Garvey (in plumed helmet) founded, were the redemption of Africa and racial self-reliance. These attracted thousands of urban Blacks in the 1920s.

Above: James Weldon Johnson's activities as educator, consular official, NAACP administrator and writer are summed up in his autobiography. *Along This Way*; his social views in *Negro Americans. What Now?*

the British West Indies and he was especially moved by the oratory of Mrs Marcus Garvey, who spoke for the Black women of Jamaica. It is certain that he felt great gratification in seeing his vision of Pan-Africanism in the well-trusted hands of Africans themselves.

The Harlem Renaissance and the Elders

The basic optimism of the 1920s is reflected in James Weldon Johnson's *Black Manhattan* (1930), a book that places great emphasis on the theatrical dimension of Black culture. It is representative of the mood of Black artists and intellectuals in New York and in other metropolitan centers at the time, and this, in turn, is representative of the Black masses – it is not too much to say that this necessarily small group and the larger Black population were more as one than is usual between artist and the person in the street.

The mood of hope and cheer that permeates Johnson's work is based upon his perception of Harlem as a cultural community with an intense life of its own, but with an outreach that had attracted international attention. A number of artists and thinkers boldly proclaimed that Harlem's creativity held the greatest promise for the renewal of all the arts, that Harlem was the crossroads of culture.

The Harlem of the twenties bound together a small group of artists and intellectuals, nearly all natives of other regions of the United States or of the British West Indies, to a large working class population of similar origins. Its life centered around the social and political clubs and lodges, the churches and, to an extent unknown in most other American communities, popular theater and music. Apart from puritans and snobbish intellectuals, a well of community sympathy existed for the great entertainers. If Harlem had a reigning divinity in the twenties it was Florence Mills, the star of *Blackbirds*. Her funeral in 1927 was the most elaborate Harlem ever saw.

Certain major figures gave the Harlem Renaissance its character. Among the elders, in relative order of seniority, are Du Bois, James Weldon Johnson, Jessie Fauset, Alain Locke, Walter White and Charles S. Johnson. It is a matter of some significance that each of these men contributed to Locke's *The New Negro*.

The elders were connected in a number of interesting ways. Du Bois and James Weldon Johnson were in their late fifties by 1925 and were well known and highly respected. Locke and Fauset, both in their late forties by then, shared a Philadelphia background; White and Charles S. Johnson, aged around 30, each occupied important posts in the leading civil rights organizations – White in the NAACP along with James Weldon Johnson, Du Bois and Fauset, and C.S. Johnson in the Urban League. White also shared an Atlanta University experience with Du Bois and J.W. Johnson, while Du Bois, Fauset and Locke had all studied extensively in Europe. By 1925, four of them had written novels, J.W. Johnson, Du Bois, Fauset and White, and Locke, Du Bois and J.W. Johnson had written on spirituals. All were enthusiastic supporters of the theater.

From the constant recurrence of the name W.E.B. Du Bois, it can be seen that for black intellectuals of the twenties he evoked an image of the highest achievement, intelligence,

Above right: Mary McLeod Bethune and W.E.B. Du Bois receiving Lincoln University Alpha Medallion Awards in 1950. Mary Bethune was the founder of Bethune-Cookman College, as well as of the National Council of Negro Women.

Mrs Bethune became an important advisor on minority affairs and an agency director in the administration of Franklin D. Roosevelt. On the right is Dr. Horace Mann Bond, who was President of Lincoln University.

and purposeful action. It was his passionate interest in the theater that tied him in most closely with the Harlem Renaissance and in 1925 he formed the Krigwa Players, a Black theater company for Harlem. He wrote frequently on the theater, as a critic, trying to raise his readers' consciousness of what is good. As a supporter, he tried to instil a sense of hope and purpose in potential actors and playwrights. His praise of such productions as *Shuffle Along* and *The Green Pastures* was crucial to the self-esteem of Black theater, as well as to the temper of the Harlem Renaissance.

James Weldon Johnson, almost the equal of Du Bois in dignity and prestige, was considered warmer and easier to know as a person. A librettist of Broadway shows at the beginning of the century, he had created the English translation of the opera *Goyescas* for the Metropolitan Opera in 1915. He was, like Du Bois, a person of action as well as poet, novelist, and playwright and had been a United States Consul in Venezuela and Nicaragua. He was Secretary of the NAACP in the twenties. His contribution to theater history in *Black Manhattan* cannot be overrated: it remains a principal source of information and inspiration. His volume of verse, *God's Trombones*, appeared in 1927. In it Johnson sought to convey the oratorical power of the old-time Black sermon, and succeeded so well that many of his poems entered the oral tradition and took on a life of their own. Johnson edited anthologies of Black poetry in 1922 and 1931, and his final contribution to poetry was the satirical *St Peter Relates an Incident of the Judgement Day* published in the 1930s.

Left and below: A superb actor, a great singer and a towering intellectual, Paul Robeson was one of the most memorable figures of the twentieth century. His appearances in *Othello* (right) are major events in the history of theater in the United States and England. Here (left), he plays The Fugitive in Eugene O'Neill's *The Emperor Jones.*

Jessie Fauset spent nearly 15 years as a French and Latin teacher after a brilliant record at Cornell University, the University of Pennsylvania, and the Sorbonne. She came to New York in 1920 to work with Du Bois on the *Crisis* as its literary editor and in 1924 she published the first of four novels set in and around her native Philadelphia. For Locke's *The New Negro*, her contribution was a milestone essay on Black comedy, *The Gift of Laughter.*

From the same Philadelphia milieu that produced Jessie Fauset came Alain Locke. After Harvard, Locke broke new ground as a Rhodes Scholar at Oxford, England, returning to become a professor at Howard University, with which he was identified for the remainder of his life. One of his first moves at Howard was to sponsor a student dramatic club. A decade later he joined with Charles S. Johnson in making the Urban League journal, *Opportunity*, a vehicle of intellectual stimulation and artistic expression. For Locke, drama was the temple of the arts and he served at its altar manifoldly as theorist, critic, editor, and animator.

Walter White, like C.S. Johnson, was only at the beginning of a long and distinguished career in the twenties. His energy seemed boundless and he was everywhere on the Harlem Renaissance scene like a cultural broker, keeping in touch with a multitude of editors, publishers, and philanthropists on behalf of the younger, and some older Black writers and artists. His blond hair and blue eyes often caused quite a sensation when, as head of the NAACP, he spoke for Black people as a Black man.

Charles S. Johnson was the first editor of *Opportunity* and later encouraged Locke's shaping of this journal, which was so basic to the development of the Harlem Renaissance. He was the initiator of the *Opportunity* Prize Contests. In 1927 he edited the anthology *Ebony and Topaz*, which deserves more credit as the adjunct to *The New Negro* than it has received. His role in fostering the talents of a number of important figures was crucial.

Hayes, Robeson, Hughes

In an exercise to select one outstanding figure from music, theater, and literature to symbolize the Harlem Renaissance, the names that come most readily to mind are Roland Hayes, Paul Robeson, and Langston Hughes. All of them were famous in their day and all have kept a well-earned place in history ever since. Portraits of them by Winold Reiss hang in the National Portrait Gallery in Washington, D.C.

In December 1923, Roland Hayes appeared in concert at New York's Town Hall and created an uproar. He was already in his mid-thirties and had made a long, arduous progress from rural poverty in Georgia to a widely applauded European concert tour. Hayes was a lyric tenor who excelled in singing *lieder* and other classical music in Italian, German, and French, but he became an instant hero of Black America for the artistry and tenderness with which he sang spirituals.

Hayes had been born into the still lingering world of the Folk-Rural Culture, of which the spiritual was a vital and vibrant part. His affectionate memory of the songs sung by his mother and her generation, who had first heard and sung them in slavery, was reflected in a life-long devotion to singing them.

Below: Zora Neale Hurston was a folklorist and anthropologist, whose fiction is characterized by the flavor of the Folk-Rural lifestyle. In *Mules and Men*, she offered the actual result of some of her folklore studies in anecdotal and dramatic manner.

Facing page: One of the most prolific Black American writers, Langston Hughes traveled widely, was consumed by a passion for human justice and dignity, and articulated in such books as his Simple books the views and aspirations of Trans-Urban Black America.

The spiritual had first been brought to the concert stage in the 1870s by the Fisk Jubilee Singers. At the beginning of the twentieth century, Harry T. Burleigh had begun to arrange spirituals for solo voice and in 1919 accompanied Hayes in a recital that included them. Following the Town Hall recital of 1923, Hayes always sang spirituals as part of his programs and thereafter these traditional songs became a permanent addition to the general recital repertory. Roland Hayes continued to perform into the early 1960s, when he gave a 75th birthday recital at Carnegie Hall.

Paul Robeson, already known as an actor, gave a concert of spirituals and other Afro-American folk songs in New York in 1925. He was a dramatic basso with a magnificent stage presence. Born in Princeton, New Jersey, he represented the Folk-Urban tradition of the spiritual as it developed in the churches of the cities following the Civil War. His interest was always more in folk songs – of Europe and Asia as well as the Americas – than in "art" songs.

Robeson had first made a name for himself as an athlete, excelling in football, baseball, and competitive sports – as a member of the football team of Rutgers University, he was chosen for the All-American Team in 1917 and 1918. At the same time he was a brilliant student, achieving the highest average of his generation at Rutgers. Robeson went on to the Columbia University School of Law from which he was graduated in 1923, but involvement in amateur drama groups drew him to the theater and he soon became a professional entertainer.

In 1924 Robeson had the lead in Eugene O'Neill's *All God's Chillun Got Wings*, a play about an interracial romance and marriage. He had already appeared in a revival of O'Neill's *The Emperor Jones*, a role that is almost synonymous with his name. It was in *The Emperor Jones* that he launched his international career on the London stage in 1925 and his film career in 1933.

Robeson was a great success in London in *Othello* in 1930, but did not play this powerful character in his own country until 1942. His singing and acting in the stage and film versions of *Show Boat* won new acclaim, and the song *Ol' Man River* became his very own. Robeson appeared in more than ten films as a star, but few of his later roles were worthy of his talents. His conversion to radical politics led to difficulties at home and he lived much of his life in self-imposed exile.

Langston Hughes came to the attention of readers of *Crisis* with his poem *The Negro Speaks of Rivers*. In 1925 he won first prize for poetry in the *Opportunity* Literary Contest, and in that same year his verse was published in *The New Negro*. His first volume of poetry, *The Weary Blues*, appeared in 1926 and propelled him to the top rank of Black American poets. He was compared to Dunbar and Sandburg, comparisons that reflect esteem and a sense of his modernism.

During the twenties Hughes left Columbia University after only a year of study to travel, turning his hand to many odd jobs, starting out as a merchant seaman, visiting Africa and then making his way around Europe by other means. On his return home, a rich patron enabled him to go back to college and he entered Lincoln University in Pennsylvania. This time he graduated, but

Below: segretation of
work, 1945 in Belle
Glade, Florida.

he also finished his novel, *Not Without Laughter*, while there.

Hughes' later career was also varied. He wrote prodigiously, lectured, gave readings of his work, traveled and occasionally taught. Having promised himself to live on his income as a writer, he kept this pledge from 1930 to his death in 1967 – Hughes always lived modestly.

In an enormous output, Hughes wrote at least 30 plays and librettos including *Mulatto* (1935), *Soul Gone Home* (1937), and *Black Nativity* (1961) as well as two volumes of autobiography, *The Big Sea* (1940) and *I Wonder As I Wander* (1956). His fiction includes two novels, three volumes of short stories, children's books, and several volumes of sketches devoted to his Harlem character, Simple. Hughes edited at least 20 books, alone or with others, and produced several history books. He also published at least 17 volumes of poetry.

With so much to recommend him to the hearts and minds of his people, Hughes is best remembered and loved as the poet whose work reflects much in the lives of ordinary Black Americans.

The Thirties

For the third of the Black American population that had settled in the cities of the North, the 1920s had been a period of guarded optimism – they even participated to some extent in the "roaring." Two-thirds of Black Americans, however, were locked into the poverty and terror of the rural South, though the Trans-Urban Culture touched them in the larger cities. The coming of the Great Depression, with its general demoralization of American life, was a particularly tragic episode for Blacks already at the bottom of the economic ladder.

An event that was symbolic of the precarious position of Blacks in the United States occurred in 1931 with the conviction of nine young men for rape in Scottsboro, Alabama. Their conviction was based on the testimony of the two white women who were the alleged victims, though one of them subsequently recanted. The jury, in a hasty trial, found all the accused guilty and recommended the death penalty for eight of them – it could not agree on the appropriate penalty for the ninth, who was just 12 years old. The United States Supreme Court overturned the verdict in 1932 on the grounds that the defendants had not had a fair trial or adequate legal representation but the state of Alabama, buttressed by local opinion, was determined to reconvict the Scottsboro boys, and did so. The case dragged on and on with the boys – growing into men – shunted in and out of prison as one side or the other made legal headway. By 1946 all had been freed except for the one pinpointed as the ringleader by the prosecution. He did not win his own freedom until 1948, when he escaped to Michigan, which refused to extradite him.

The Scottsboro case brought protests from foes of injustice all around the world. At home in 1933 a March on Washington was organized, and 3000 people participated. President Franklin D. Roosevelt refused to meet the organizing committee, possibly because it included members of the Communist Party. (It is true that the Communists had made propaganda use of the case, but many felt that the President was being more careful not to offend his white Southern supporters.)

Pvt. Joe Louis says—

"We're going to do our part ...and we'll win because we're on God's side"

Above: This patriotic poster from World War II uses "Pvt. Joe Louis" to recruit Blacks into the armed forces.

Despite this, President Roosevelt was winning Black loyalties by then through New Deal measures that, however minimally, were helping them. In 1936 they joined the rest of the nation in returning him to the White House. Many of the public works projects of the New Deal included Blacks, if on a segregated basis – one of the most successful was the Works Progress Administration (WPA). The WPA reached into almost every economic sector of the Black community. It was much better known than the Federal Art, Writers' and Theater Projects, which were to prove so important for Black painters, authors, musicians, and performers.

World War II

The United States' declaration of war following the December 1941 Japanese attack on Pearl Harbor called forth a patriotic response from Black Americans. Despite the injustice, humiliation, and outright cruelty that held them down, they joined the armed forces in great numbers.

In a memorable 1941 speech, President Roosevelt had opened up a vision of a world in which everyone would enjoy freedom of expression, freedom of worship, freedom from want, and freedom from fear. These Four Freedoms were later adopted as the war aims of the Allies. Blacks, however, could not help noticing the discrepancy between the resounding wartime slogans and their own condition in real life.

It was in the climate of the world's hope for the Four Freedoms that A. Philip Randolph, the distinguished and scholarly Black labor leader, called for a March on Washington to open up employment opportunities in defense industries. It was to take place in July 1941. A few days before the event, President Roosevelt issued the first Fair Employment order ever promulgated in the United States, prohibiting discrimination in war-support jobs. Problems and impediments marred the implementation of the order, but it was welcomed by Blacks South and North.

As in World War I, Black migration from the South multiplied, and this time a considerable number went to the West Coast. The new migration created strong tensions that fired wartime race riots. The ugly fact of segregation in the armed

Below: Black soldiers contribute to the war effort during World War II. Here soldiers test a jeep-mounted mortar.

forces also inflamed Blacks both in and out of the services although despite this more than half a million saw wartime service.

At the war's end, the overall mood of Black Americans was hopeful. And this optimism seemed well-founded when, in 1946, President Harry S. Truman appointed a Committee on Civil Rights with a brief to inquire into the grievances of Blacks and to propose solutions.

Desegregation

In 1954 the Supreme Court ruled unanimously in a school segregation case, *Brown vs. The Board of Education* (of Topeka), that separate educational facilities were "inherently illegal." In so doing, the court reversed the decision of 1896 that had established the legal basis for the "separate but equal" edifice of segregation. The ruling was greeted with enthusiasm by Black Americans who joyfully anticipated the rapid ending of segregation in other walks of life. Their joy was rapidly dampened.

White reaction to the decision was ominous, Southern opposition to school desegregation took many forms, some of them violent, and most Southerners pledged themselves to "massive resistance." At the national level, 101 members of congress from the South signed a Southern Manifesto in 1956 that proclaimed that they would resist desegregation by every means.

Martin Luther King, Jr. and Civil Rights

In the face of white intransigence, groups of Blacks formed to press for the elimination of segregation in the South. One of the most notable and successful of these efforts was the Montgomery Bus Boycott, organized

Below: Josephine Eli registers as one of the first Black students at Louisiana State University, 1958.

Right: Desegregation begins. Bruce Alvin Roberts entered an all-white primary school for the first time in Dallas 1961.

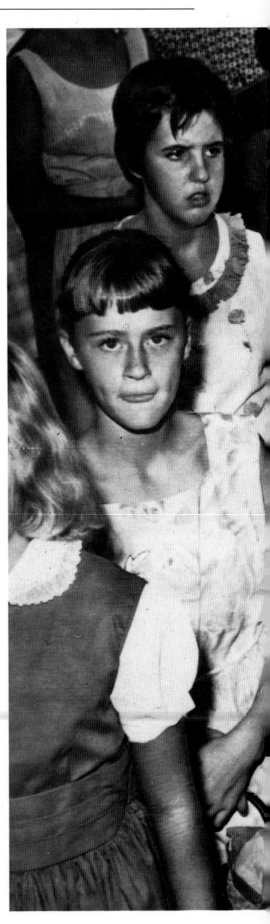

Facing page: James
Farmer, the director
of the Congress of
Racial Equality, sits
at a previously only-
white lunch counter
in Montgomery bus
station, 1961.
National Guardsmen
on the right were
called out on duty
after martial law was
declared.

Above: Racial
clashes in Mont-
gomery, Alabama,
1960. An unidenti-
fied white man is
caught by the pho-
tographer as he
draws back to strike
a 22-year-old Black
girl. No arrests were
made.

to protest against segregation in public transport in Alabama. It introduced the teachings of one of the most charismatic Black civil rights leaders of his time, Martin Luther King.

The Montgomery Boycott, based on the principle of non-violence, was launched in late 1955; by mid-1956 King had become an international celebrity. His reputation rested on a remarkable ability to organize and on a powerful personality unusual in one so young (he was only 26 years old). King was a graduate of Morehouse College and held a Ph.D. in Theology from Boston University. He had absorbed the ideas of a host of philosophers and theologians from antiquity on down, drawing on them to formulate a philosophical link to questions of public morality. In this pursuit he had read and was influenced by the teachings of Thoreau and Gandhi.

While it is clear that King did not accept his pastorate in Montgomery with immediate civil rights activity in mind, circumstances thrust him into action. He was ready. In a speech in Montgomery in December 1956, he voiced his belief in the laws as a means of change:

We must continue to struggle
through legalism and
legislation. There are those
who contend that integration
can come only through
education, for no other reason
than that morals cannot be
legislated. I choose, however,
to be dialectical at this point.
It is neither education nor
legislation; it is both legislation
and education. I quite agree
that it is impossible to change
a man's internal feelings
merely through law. But this

Previous pages: Dr. Martin Luther King, Jr. in a characteristic pose – his spirit of non-violence lives on today.

Above and below: Blacks and white-robed Ku Klux Klansmen picket Atlanta's largest department store in 1960.

Facing page: Black students sit on the pavement as high pressure hoses are turned on their backs during a demonstration against racial segregation in Birmingham, Alabama, 1963.

Facing page, inset: A member of NAACP, Robert Carter signs the register at a motel in Jackson Mississippi, 1964, when segregation barriers were lifted following the passing as law of the Civil Rights Bill.

really is not the intention of
the law. The law does not seek
to change one's internal
feelings; it seeks rather to
control the external effects of
those internal feelings. For
instance, the law cannot make
a man love – religion and
education must do that – but it
can control his efforts to lynch.
So in order to control the external
effects of prejudiced internal
feelings, we must continue to
struggle through legislation.

The methods of the struggle pro-
posed by King were non-violence
and passive resistance:

... if we are to speed up the
coming of the new age we must
have the moral courage to
stand up and protest against
injustice wherever we find it.
Wherever we find segregation
we must have the fortitude to
passively resist it. I realize that
this will mean suffering and
sacrifice. It might even mean
going to jail. If such is the case
we must be willing to fill up
the jail houses of the South.
It might even mean physical
death. But if physical death is
the price that some must pay
to free their children from a
permanent life of psychological
death, then nothing could be
more honorable. Once more it
might well turn out that the
blood of the martyr will be the
seed of the tabernacle of freedom.

King was committed not only to
resisting social evil by non-violence,
but also to establishing a community
based on mutual respect and love for
the "Beloved Community":

Below: A white youth matches strides with a Black student picketing Woolworth's in Greensboro, north Carolina during the lunch counter sit-down demonstration. The movement to seek equality of service in eating places which swept the South originated in Greensboro, 1960.

Facing page: In a light moment during the historic Washington civil rights demonstration, Mrs Johnson fell into the pool while taking a photograph of the scene. Note the massive parade of demonstrators in the background.

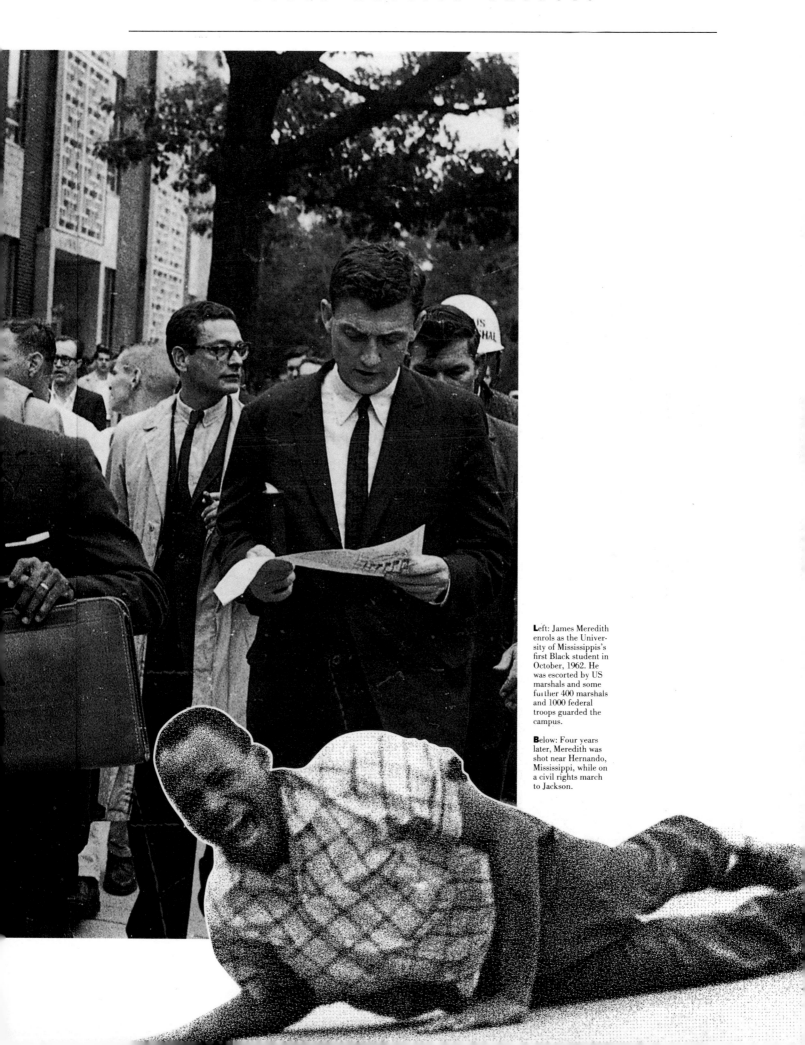

Left: James Meredith enrols as the University of Mississippi's first Black student in October, 1962. He was escorted by US marshals and some further 400 marshals and 1000 federal troops guarded the campus.

Below: Four years later, Meredith was shot near Hernando, Mississippi, while on a civil rights march to Jackson.

CXVII.No. 40,249

© 1968 The New York Times Company.

The New York Times

NEW YORK, FRIDAY, APRIL 5, 1968

MARTIN LUTHER KING IS SLAIN IN
WHITE IS SUSPECTED; JOHNSON U

**DELAYS
AWAIT;
TODAY**

Hanoi Charges U.S. Raid
Far North of 20th Parallel

By EVERT CLARK
Special to The New York Times

WASHINGTON, April 4—
North Vietnam charged in a broadcast today that United States planes had bombed a "populated area" in northwestern Vietnam far north of the 20th parallel. The Defense Department said it knew of no such raid but was investigating.

President Johnson has ordered that there be no attacks on North Vietnam north of the 20th Parallel as a step toward de-escalating the war.

[In South Vietnam, United States marines beat off an attack by about 400 North Vietnamese soldiers charging up a hill near Khesanh, killing 93, The Associated Press reported. Meanwhile, an American relief column was nearing the besieged base. Page 15.]

The Hanoi radio, in a broadcast monitored and translated, said three waves of United States planes dropped more than 50 bombs on a "popu-

Continued on Page 15, Column 1

**Hanoi said that area near
Laichau (cross) was target.**

lated area" about 30 miles west of Laichau, capital of Laichau Province, this morning. The nearest village to that

DISMAY IN NATION

**Negroes Urge Others
to Carry on Spirit
of Nonviolence**

By LAWRENCE VAN GELDER

Dismay, shame, anger and foreboding marked the nation's reaction last night to the Rev. Dr. Martin Luther King Jr.'s murder.

From the high offices of state to the man in the street, news of the moderate civil rights leader's violent death in Memphis yesterday drew, for the most part, stunned and sober statements.

Most major Negro organizations and Negro leaders, lamenting Dr. King's death, expressed hope that it serve as a spur to others to carry on in his spirit of nonviolence. But some Negro militants responded with bitterness and anger.

Roy Wilkins, executive director of the National Association for the

PRESIDENT'S PLEA

**On TV, He Deplores
'Brutal' Murder of
Negro Leader**

*Statements by Johnson and
Humphrey are on Page 24.*

Special to The New York Times

WASHINGTON, April 4—President Johnson deplored tonight in a brief television address to the nation the "brutal" slaying" of the Rev. Dr. Martin Luther King Jr.

He asked "every citizen to reject the blind violence that has struck Dr. King, who lived by nonviolence."

Mr. Johnson said he was postponing his scheduled departure tonight for a conference on

**PHREY HINTS
L ENTER RACE**

**Johnson Shuns Rele
Of '68 'Le**

THE REV. DR. MARTIN LUTHER KING Jr.

Associated Press

Scattered Violence Occurs
In Harlem and Brooklyn

Previous pages, left: Over 200,000 people turned out to mark the twentieth anniversary of the 1963 demonstration in which Dr. Martin Luther King Jr. delivered his "I have a dream" speech.

Previous pages, right: Dr. Martin Luther King (left) and Black Muslim leader Malcolm X (right) meet in Washington in March 1964. Malcolm X was assassinated in 1965 and Dr. King in 1968.
The Nobel Peace Prize crowned Dr. King's efforts for a non-violent solution to the problem of human dignity posed by legally sanctioned racial discrimination in the United States.

Facing page: Martin Luther King stands on the balcony at the Lorraine Motel with aides a day before he was killed.

Above and inset: *The New York Times* lead story covers the assassination.

Left: The assassination aftermath – Washington DC was witness to looting and arson in the wake of the assassination of Dr. Martin Luther King, in April 1968.

Facing page: Having worked closely with her husband throughout his participation in the Civil Rights movement, Coretta Scott King committed herself to continue and extend his teaching through the establishment of the Martin Luther King Jr. Center for Non-Violent Social Change in Atlanta.

Left: An aide to Dr. King, later a Congressman, then the United States Ambassador to the United States, Andrew Young is sought out for his views and support by people and organizations all over the world.

If we will join together in doing all of these things we will be able to speed up the coming of the new World – a new world in which men will live together as brothers; a world in which men will beat their swords into ploughshares and their spears into pruninghooks; a world in which men will no longer take necessities from the masses to give luxuries to the classes; a world in which all men will respect the dignity and worth of all human personality.

One of the highpoints of King's achievement was the March on Washington of 1963. His *I Have A Dream* speech, an eloquent evocation of the Beloved Community, moved millions the world over. Most of the other leading figures of the civil rights movement were also in Washington for the march, including Roy Wilkins of the NAACP, Whitney Young of the National Urban League, and John Lewis of the Student Non-Violent Coordinating Committee (SNCC). James Farmer, Director of the Congress of Racial Equality (CORE) was absent, having been arrested during a demonstration in Louisiana. Also absent was Malcolm X, who had emerged as a dynamic opponent to King and to the traditional Black leadership.

A series of Civil Rights Acts and the Voting Rights Act of 1965 owed their existence to the Civil Rights movement. Improved opportunities in education, elimination of much overt discrimination, and a host of other changes have come about since the Montgomery Boycott, but the dream of Martin Luther King still remains unfulfilled.

Above: John H. Johnson is the successful head of Johnson Publications, a multimillion dollar corporation which produces five magazines, including *Ebony*.

Left and facing page: After the death of Dr. King, Jesse Jackson established Operation PUSH in Chicago, from which he launched a succession of uplift endeavours, including a bid for the nomination as presidential candidate of the Democratic Party in 1984 and 1988.

Left: The King family honor Dr. Martin Luther King. Appearing on the steps of the Lincoln Memorial are Martin Luther King Senior and Martin Luther King III.

Facing page: A former police officer, a genial politician and an extremely popular mayor of Los Angeles, Tom Bradley narrowly missed being elected Governor of California, because of the racial biases of some of his fellow citizens.

Left: During several terms as a congresswoman from Brooklyn, Shirley Chisholm became one of the best-known women politicians in the United States, mounting a much publicized campaign for the presidency in 1972.

African Diaspora

The African Diaspora – the Black peoples living outside Africa in scattered settlements throughout the Americas – took hold of the Black American consciousness as post-war African countries asserted their nationhood.

Interest in Africa had long existed among United States Blacks, stimulated by Pan-African Congresses, the Garvey movement, and the New Negro emphasis on African origins. Recognition of the African Diaspora consolidated the link to those origins and inspired a sense of community with the Blacks of the rest of the Western hemisphere.

The English-speaking Caribbean once had close links with English-speaking North America, but these were broken by the American Revolution. In spite of this, some North American Blacks had occasional contact with Blacks from the islands before the Civil War. Late in the nineteenth century an influx of Black West Indians and Bahamians started, reaching a crescendo in the 1920s – at that time, newcomers from the West Indies made up one fourth of the population of Harlem. Claude McKay and Marcus Garvey were two such immigrants who made an impact on their new homeland; both had originally been drawn by Tuskegee, but eventually found their destiny in New York City.

There was a smaller entry of Blacks from the Spanish-speaking areas of the Caribbean: Puerto Rico, Cuba, and the Dominican Republic. In New York City this incoming population created Spanish Harlem.

The consciousness of the African Diaspora increased in the post-World War II decades when attention focused on the existence of Black, but largely suppressed and inarticulate, populations in Latin America. A scholarly basis for the appreciation and understanding of the African Diaspora had been laid by the researches of the anthropologist Melville Herskovits. His book, *The Myth of the Negro Past*, made a stir when it appeared in 1941. W.E.B. Du Bois wholeheartedly approved of the book. Herskovits' body of work included several books on folk life in Surinam, Haiti, Trinidad, and Dahomey.

Communication among scholars and writers of Africa and the African Diaspora was nutured by the journal *Présence Africaine*, edited in Paris by Alioune Diop, in a series of conferences beginning in 1956. Ten years later a world festival celebrating Africa and the Diaspora was held in Dakar, Senegal, under the patronage of President Sedar Senghor, himself a poet and scholar. In 1977 another such celebration was held in Lagos, Nigeria.

In the late 1970s Professor Joseph Harris of Howard University organized two African Diaspora conferences, the first at Howard, the second at the University of Nairobi in Kenya. Harris edits the *African Diaspora Newsletter*. Under the sponsorship of the Center for African and African-American Studies of Atlanta University, Richard A. Long organized a series of New World Festivals of the African Diaspora, which were held in Brazil (1978), Haiti (1979), Surinam (1982), and Barbados (1985).

Black Vernacular English

Every culture has its language, and the Black American culture, past and present, is no exception – there have been dialects of the Folk-Rural, the

Folk-Urban, and the Trans-Urban Cultures. Discussion of these languages or dialect variations has always been controversial.

In an influential paper of 1971 entitled *Towards A Theory of Afro-American Dialect*, Richard A. Long suggested the term Black Vernacular English (BVE) for the varieties of Trans-Urban speech to substitute for the term Black English, which was offensive to some Black people. BVE was thereafter occasionally used by some linguists as more acceptable. Recently, the term Black English has stirred less resentment since it is taken to refer to ghetto English as opposed to standard Black usage.

The dialect of the Folk-Rural Culture is the ancestor of, but not identical with, the varieties of BVE spoken by the young in today's urban ghettos. Both the history and structure of BVE have been the preoccupation of a number of scholars, some of whom have addressed themselves to the social implications of the use and perpetuation of the dialect. Such scholars participated in a court case in Ann Arbor in which the responsibility of a public school system to speakers of the dialect was defined.

Black Poetry

The character of the outpouring of verse during the Harlem Renaissance may be appreciated in the poets whom Locke selected for the volume *Four Negro Poets*, a collection illustrating aspects of American culture. The poets were Claude McKay, Jean Toomer, Countee Cullen, and Langston Hughes.

Claude McKay, born in Jamaica and already the author of two volumes of poems in Jamaican Creole before he came to the United States in his twenties, was the oldest of Locke's writers. He published *Spring in New Hampshire* in England in 1920 and *Harlem Shadows* in 1922. His poems are traditional in technique and on the sentimental side in subject and tone. He became widely known, to his own despair, for a single poem called *If We Must Die*, which was perceived as a statement of racial defiance. Many have proclaimed the poem universal, and the British statesman Winston Churchill is said to have quoted it as an expression of defiance to the Nazis during World War II. McKay himself always insisted that it was a proletarian poem, the "mad and hungry dogs" referred to being the goons of the capitalists, not lynch mobs. The poem, a Shakespearean sonnet in form, made a great impact on Black America.

In the volume *Cane*, which contained stories and poems of wistful melancholy, Jean Toomer made a strong entrance on the stage of Black American literature. His subsequent writing took other directions and, by 1931, Toomer himself was no longer sure that he was a Black poet. Nonetheless his poem, *Song of the Son*, had found a secure place in the Black culture. Its concluding stanzas are:

O Negro slaves, dark purple
    ripened plums,
Squeezed and bursting in the pine-
    wood air,
Passing, before they stripped the
    old tree bare
One plum was saved for me, one
    seed becomes

An everlasting song, a singing tree,
Caroling softly souls of slavery,
What they were, and what they are
    to me,
Caroling softly souls of slavery.

Below: Born in Jamaica, and spending much of the 1920s in Europe and north Africa, Claude McKay nevertheless wrote essentially American books, the best known of which is the novel *Home to Harlem.*

Countee Cullen was prolific in the twenties, publishing three volumes of poems. Always traditional in his technique and even in his poetic themes, his poems won many admirers by their special kind of verbal harmony. The usual reaction to a Cullen poem was "it's beautiful." These lines are from *To Keats, Poet At Springtime:*

I cannot hold my peace, John
  Keats;
There never was a spring like this;
  It is an echo, that repeats
My least year's song and next year's
  bliss.
And you and I, shall we lie still,
John Keats, while Beauty summons
  us?

There was at bottom a deep melancholy in the soul and art of Cullen, nowhere more poignant than in the final couplet of his sonnet, *Yet Do I Marvel:*

Yet do I marvel at this curious
  thing:
To make a poet black, and bid him
  sing!

Langston Hughes is the only one of the four who continued writing poetry into the 1960s, again and again producing poems that seemed to speak directly to the concerns of the day while fitting into the overall body of his work. He differed from the other three in two important ways. First, he consciously drew his inspiration directly from everyday folk and their speech, and second, he utilized non-traditional techniques, free verse, and the blues.

Hughes' quality of spirit are well expressed in the second stanza of his poem, *Dream Variations:*

To fling my arms wide
In the face of the sun,
Dance! Whirl! Whirl!
Till the quick day is done.
Rest at pale evening . . .
A tall, slim tree . . .
Night coming tenderly
Black like me.

There were a great many other black poets at work in this era and later. Two whose verse first appeared in the twenties and who continued on the scene for decades after are Arna Bontemps and Sterling Brown. Bontemps worked in more traditional styles, approaching Cullen in mood but with a more philosophical bent. Brown was closer to Langston Hughes' terrain, speaking of and in the manner of the folk.

Above: One of the most powerful writers of the twentieth century, James Baldwin has attained mastery both in fiction and in the essay. His work for the theater is important and the play *The Amen Corner* is a staple of Black Community theater.

Below: As an example of realistic fiction, Richard Wright's *Native Son* created a sensation when it appeared. Shortly after the quasi-autobiographical *Black Boy* was published, Wright became the outstanding delineator of the defiant Black. He moved, however, to France and produced a very different kind of fiction in *The Outsider*, and then turned to interpretative accounts of his travels.

Black Fiction and Literary Autobiography

Jean Toomer's *Cane* in 1923 was the herald of Harlem Renaissance fiction and was recognized as such by the critic William Stanley Braithwaite in the concluding paragraph of his 1924 essay, *The Negro in American Literature:*

Finally in Jean Toomer the author of *Cane*, we come upon the very first artist of the race, who with all an artist's passion and sympathy for life, its hurts, its sympathies, its desires, its joys, its defeats and strange yearnings, can write about the Negro without the surrender or compromise of the artist's vision. So objective is it, that we feel that it is a mere accident that birth or association has thrown him into contact with the life he has written about. He would write just as well, just as poignantly, just as transmutingly, about the peasants of Russia, or the peasants of Ireland, had experience brought him in touch with their existence. *Cane* is a book of gold and bronze, of dust and flame, of ecstasy and pain, and Jean Toomer is a bright morning star of a new day of the race of literature.

Before saying this, Braithwaite reviewed the earlier fiction of Dunbar and Charles Waddell Chesnutt, classifying the former as a "sentimentalist" and the latter as a "realist." Dunbar had died in 1902 and Chesnutt had not published since 1905, so *Cane* marked a distinct beginning for Black writers. Almost immediately after came Walter White's *The Fire in the Flint*, an instructional novel about lynching, and Jessie Fauset's first novel, *There Is Confusion.*

Fauset's novel deals with the perplexities of middle-class Blacks in the face of racial problems. Her later novels, *Plum Bun* (1929), *The China-berry Tree* (1931), and *Comedy: American Style* (1933), amplify these topics. She was partly moved to take up the false simplicity of Blacks and Black life presented by white novelists.

It is not easy to dismiss as oversimplified the most sensational twenties novel about Blacks by a white. This was *Nigger Heaven* (1926) by Carl Van Vechten, a portrayal of Harlem life. Black opinion was split: James Weldon Johnson approved the work, Du Bois found it offensive. Young Langston Hughes was involved by providing the lyrics for the blues songs that were cited in the novel. Van Vechten included lurid details, but his intent was to give a favorable picture of intelligent and interesting Blacks and many of the characters were based on real people who were not offended by their fictional treatment.

Other Black writers of fiction in the twenties and thirties include Nella Larsen, Rudolph Fisher, and Zora Neale Hurston. Claude McKay and Langston Hughes were equally well known as poets.

Although McKay was not living in the United States for most of the twenties, he wrote *Home to Harlem* in 1928. This novel attracted some derogatory criticism because of its treatment of urban low life. His novel *Banjo* (1929), set in Marseilles, depicts the life of Black stevedores from the United States, the Caribbean, and Africa – a kind of proletarian Pan-Africanism, while *Banana Bottom* (1933), his third novel, is set in his native Jamaica. McKay's volume of short stories, *Gingertown*, was published in 1932.

Nella Larsen and Rudolph Fisher are lesser talents. Larsen shared the concerns of Fauset in presenting middle-class Blacks beset by domestic problems and troubled by the problem of color. Fisher, who had a penchant for the comic as well as the pathetic, depicts the Harlem of ordinary people in two novels and in short stories.

Langston Hughes and Zora Neale Hurston, whose lives interweave, shared an interest in Black folk life. Their literary association began in 1924, at which time he was writing poetry and she fiction. Hughes was the first to publish a novel, however, the semi-autobiographical *Not Without Laughter* (1930). His protagonist is traced from boyhood to young manhood, doing and seeing things such as Hughes himself had experienced or observed. In 1934 Hughes published a rich collection of short stories, *The Ways of White Folks*, in which cynicism, satire, and compassion engage the emotions in turn.

Hurston's novels have Southern Folk-Rural settings. *Their Eyes Were Watching God* (1937) is a complex novel of female character development in a male-dominated world, while *Jonah's Gourd Vine* (1934)

Above: W.H. Johnson moved from academic painting, through expressionism, to a final magisterial "folk" idiom at the tragic end of his career.

Below: Author Alice Walker – one of her best-known novels is *The Color Purple*.

Facing page: Ossie Davis and Ruby Dee appearing both as a husband and wife team and individually, on stage, screen and television, have a unique position in American theater. They both write and Ossie Davis has directed drama in all media. Their commitment to social action characterizes their choices of roles, to which they always bring the highest sensitivity.

and *Moses, Man of the Mountain* (1939) are shaped by her folklore research. A non-fiction work on folklore, though treated in a very personal manner, was *Mules and Men* (1935). Hurston studied folklore in Jamaica and Haiti too, and wrote about it in *Tell My Horse*, another example of her way of using literary heightening in factual writing. Hurston's autobiography, *Dust Tracks on a Road*, appeared in 1942.

Hughes had a gift for Folk-Urban portrayal, which came to full fruition in his creation of Jesse B. Simple, the hero of a succession of books beginning with *Simple Speaks His Mind*.

The remarkable talent of Richard Wright was first revealed in the powerful novellas collected as *Uncle Tom's Children* (1938). These often harrowing tales are of deep psychological complexity and profound social consciousness, but the writing style is direct and appealing. His novel, *Lawd Today*, written at the same time, was not published until after his death. Wright made an even stronger impact on the American public with *Native Son* in 1940. This novel has a permanent place in classic American literature and was the basis of Wright's international reputation. In 1945 he published an equally powerful autobiographical work, *Black Boy*. The first part of a longer work, published as *American Hunger*, *Black Boy* had been sketched out in a shorter version some years before.

Ralph Ellison, who knew Wright when *Native Son* appeared, reflects their encounter in *Invisible Man* (1952). Ellison chose a broader setting for his protagonist and used a variety of literary tools for shaping him. A number of younger Black writers have tried to reach the same

goal as Ellison.

James Baldwin was immediately proclaimed as Ellison's heir on the appearance of his first novel, *Go Tell It on the Mountain* (1953). In a succession of novels, Baldwin explored themes of Black life in conflict with the American ethos although *Giovanni's Room* (1956), is entirely different, with a European setting and white characters. Baldwin was also well known for his philosophical essays, beginning with the collection *Notes of a Native Son* (1955).

If Baldwin took over from Ellison, John O. Killins is the next in line to Wright. Both highly thought of and influential, Killins writes in the tradition of realism. His two best-known novels are *Youngblood* (1954) and *And Then We Heard the Thunder* (1963).

The autobiography has several voices. There is what may be called the "writer's autobiography," illustrated by Hughes and Hurston, and the autobiography of the public figure – the three distinguished early NAACP officials, all creative writers as well as social activists, wrote autobiographies in the "public mode." James Weldon Johnson tells the story of his life in *Along This Way* (1933); Du Bois attempts to chronicle the emergence of his philosophical and political consciousness in *Dusk of Dawn* (1940), and Walter White sticks close to his role in the NAACP in *A Man Called White*.

A third type, called autonomous autobiography, has been developed by the gifted poet and novelist Maya Angelou. Beginning with the story of her girlhood in *I Know Why the Caged Bird Sings*, she has woven a narrative more fascinating than any fiction, telling of a life as a singer, dancer, wife, mother, social and pol-

itical activist, actress and playwright. The autobiographical literature created by Angelou is unique in American writing.

With Angelou, a remarkable group of Black women writers have appeared since the late sixties, including Toni Cade Bambara, Toni Morrison, and Alice Walker. Bambara is known primarily for her short stories, though her densely written novel, *The Salt Easters*, has many devotees. Morrison has been highly praised for several novels including *Sula* and *Song of Solomon*. Walker is a poet, short story writer, and novelist, whose *The Color Purple* was a bestseller.

Paule Marshall is an extremely painstaking literary artist. The success of her *Praisesong for the Widow* prompted the reprinting of several earlier works, including *Brown Girl, Brownstones*.

While Black female writers have almost overshadowed men since the sixties, there are several male fiction writers of note. They include Ernest Gaines, who writes of rural Louisiana, James McPherson, a short story writer of penetrating insight, and John Wideman, who ranges over a variety of themes. Standing a little apart is the brilliant satirist Ishmael Reed, whose novels teem with historical allusions decorating a framework of such traditional types as the movie western, the slave narrative, and the detective story.

Alain Locke dominated Black literary criticism from the mid-twenties until his death in 1954. Other literary critics who were tastemakers for the Black reading public are Sterling Brown and Saunders Redding. A younger group includes Albert Murray, Hoyt Fuller, Addison Gayle, and Darwin Turner.

More recently yet, academic critics such as Robert Stepto, Eleanor Traylor, Houston Baker, and Eugenia Collier have come into prominence.

Black Visual Art

From the beginning of the twentieth century, the figure of Henry Ossawa Tanner, expatriate painter in Paris, towered over the Black art scene. Tanner, unable to gain acceptance as a Black painter in the United States, was able to gain acceptance as an American painter in France. Winner of a prize in the Paris Salon, he worked in the "oriental" tradition of French art, but using modern technique. His chief subject was scenes from the Bible. Tanner, who died in 1937, was held in honor back home, and many visitors to Paris sought him out.

While respecting Tanner's achievement, Alain Locke began in the twenties to call young Black artists to a deeper "ancestralism" to learn the lessons of African art, which had already influenced many European artists of reputation such as Picasso and Modigliani. Locke gently reproved Tanner's successors, such as Laura Wheeler Waring, May Howard Jackson, and William E. Harper, for not being more daring in their subject matter and technique. He applauded the young Aaron Douglas, whose work first appeared in the *New Negro* and who later provided illustrations for books such as James Weldon Johnson's *God's Trombones*. Douglas also painted murals for the Harlem YMCA.

At the appearance of the sculptor Richmond Barthe around 1930, Locke felt sure that his hope of creating a school of ancestralism had been fulfilled. One of Barthe's most

Above: Each of Toni Morrison's novels, from *The Bluest Eye* to *Beloved*, has been acclaimed a triumph of luminous craft and inspiration.

Facing page: A pupil of Eakins in Philadelphia and of Constant in Paris, Henry O. Tanner developed into a completely original artist concentrating on scenes drawn from the Bible, painted in sombre tones, accented by warm yellow and gold tints.

Following pages, left: Richmond Barthe, *The Blackberry Woman*, 1932. Bronze. 34 × 11½ inches. Collection of the Whitney Museum of American Art.

Following pages, right: Jacob Lawrence, *Tombstones*, 1942. Gouache, 28¾ × 20½ inches. Collection of the Whitney Museum of American Art.

famous works is a monumental sculpture of Toussaint L'Ouverture, which was commissioned by The Haitian government.

Two painters who started out in the twenties and became major figures in Afro-American art are W.H. Johnson and Hale Woodruff.

Johnson, born in South Carolina, underwent extreme hardship to study art in New York. After New York he went to France where he quickly absorbed the lessons of French Expressionism and he later lived and worked in Scandinavia, returning home in the late thirties. He was forced to stop working by mental illness in the mid-1940s. Johnson's art underwent changes in style, motivated usually by his circumstances and surroundings: the academic paintings of his New York student days were followed by the expressionist paintings of his days in the South of France, while his Scandinavian period was different again, followed by a folk period recalling the rural South of his youth.

Woodruff took his academic training in art in Indianapolis and then he also went to France to study and paint. He returned to the United States to teach art, first at Atlanta University and later at New York University. He moved from painting subjects of Southern regionalism to more abstract works, often inspired by African legendary and religious symbols in this he approached Locke's dreamed-of ancestralism. Woodruff also painted important murals, in part inspired by studies in Mexico. The most famous are the *Amistad Mutiny* at Talledega College and *The Art of the Negro* at Atlanta University.

Beginning in the late twenties, a group of talented artists taught at Howard University in the Art Department under the chairmanship of James Vernon Herring. James Porter, who later succeeded Herring, was a painter and an art historian. James Lessesne Wells was an outstanding graphic artist. Lois Mailou Jones (Mme. Pierre Noel) has enjoyed an enduring career as a multifaceted artist, producing major works reflecting her residence in France, Haiti and elsewhere.

A Mexican connection can also be traced in the work of Charles White, Elizabeth Catlett, and Margaret Burroughs, who appear in the 1940s. White worked almost exclusively in charcoal, creating powerful drawings and prints in black and white. He was always in search of expression for his profound and deeply felt social consciousness, and he set an example that was followed by some activist artists of the 1960s. Catlett, working primarily in sculpture but also in prints, depicted heroic and triumphant Black women. Margaret Burroughs, poet and political activist, devoted her talent to the depiction of Black history.

Beauford Delaney operated a little apart from the mainstream of Black American art, but he was always deeply sensitive to the work of the other artists. Delaney went from his birthplace in Kentucky to Boston for several years of study. At the end of the twenties he came to New York and began a massive portrait portfolio of Black American types and celebrities, worked in charcoal and pastel. Over the next 20 years he developed a bold expressionist style in creating cityscapes and theatrical scenes. Delaney went to Paris in the early 1950s. While never losing interest in portraiture, he succeeded in developing a lyrical non-objective

style in rendering the effects of light on surfaces.

The most precocious of the Black painters was Jacob Lawrence, who had achieved national fame by his early twenties. The works that made his name were the narrative sequences, *Toussaint L'Ouverture* and *Migration,* which are painted in gouache, in a cubist technique of solid-colored planes. Lawrence concentrates on urban subjects with sharp social content, not moving far from the stylistic domain he established in his youth.

In contrast, Romare Bearden continually experimented in medium, style, and content. He is best known for his work in collage and has been recognized as one of the best in this medium. His subjects have included the Greek classic *Iliad* and bullfight scenes in his cubist mode; jazz and blues subjects in oil and water monoprint and urban, rural and Caribbean scenes in collage. He has also worked the *Odyssey* in collage. Editions of prints based on the collages are an important part of his output. Both Lawrence and Bearden span the period from the 1940s to the 1980s, and remain at the top.

In the fifties and early sixties, many Black artists were working in abstract or expressionist styles. Outstanding among these are the Chicago sculptor Richard Hunt and the Washington painter Sam Gilliam. The sixties also at last produced a wide interest in ancestralism which brought some artists to work together. An outstanding group of this kind is Africobra, originally based in Chicago. Many Africobra artists joined in creating the street wall mural, *The Wall of Respect.* Such murals have become a mark of the Trans-Urban Culture.

Black Composers

At the dawn of the twentieth century, three excellent Black composers were at work in Black America: Scott Joplin, Harry T. Burleigh, and Will Marion Cook. Joplin, best known for his ragtime music, also composed two operas, one of which, *Tree-monisha*, did not receive its first professional performance until 1972. That production in Atlanta was organized by Wendell Whalum and T.J. Anderson, staged by Katherine Dunham, and conducted by Robert Shaw. Burleigh, an excellent baritone singer, devoted himself chiefly to the composition of "art" songs and the arrangement of spirituals for solo voice. Cook, a violinist, wrote scores for many musicals and composed music for orchestras that he formed and conducted.

W.C. Handy, credited with popularizing the blues, was an instrumentalist and band conductor who composed marches and other music. He also established a music publishing company in an attempt to reach the public with his and other black composers' work.

Spirituals and folk music played an important part in the creative output of most Black composers of the twenties and thirties. Among women composers, Eva Jessye is known for arrangements of spirituals, though her reputation is at least as firmly based on her conducting skills. She was choral conductor for Thompson's opera, *Four Saints in Three Acts* (1934), and George Gershwin's *Porgy and Bess*. Florence Price composed many orchestral works, art songs, and instrumental music.

R. Nathaniel Dett is a composer who used the spiritual as a basis for larger forms, including the motet *Listen to the Lambs* and the oratorio *The Ordering of Moses*. While choral director at Hampton Institute, Dett reedited the famous volume of spirituals that was first published there in the nineteenth century. His other works include the piano suite *From the Bottoms*.

Another composer whose career is associated with a college is John W. Work III of Fisk University, son and grandson of choral conductors. Work collected and arranged Black folksongs, but also composed art songs and larger orchestral pieces. Some of these were based on his research of the music of Haiti.

Arranging spirituals was part of the output of composer Hall Johnson, who was also a choral conductor, mostly for the New York theater – he was responsible for the singing in *The Green Pastures* and for his own *Run Lil Chillin*. Johnson also appeared as a singer and actor in a number of plays.

While William L. Dawson is praised for his vigorous choral arrangements of spirituals, his fame came as a composer when his *Negro Folk Symphony* was premiered in 1933 by the Philadelphia Symphony under Leopold Stokowski. In the 1950s Dawson revised the symphony after a trip to Africa, and the new version was recorded by Stokowski.

One of the most honored Black American composers is William Grant Still, who composed his *Afro-American Symphony* in 1931. His opera of 1938, *Troubled Island*, has a libretto by Langston Hughes. A later opera was *Highway No.1 USA*. Still, who had a background in jazz as well as formal classical music study with Varese, also composed the music for the ballet, *La Guiablesse*, which was commissioned for the Chi-

Previous page: Charles White, *Preacher*, 1952. Ink on Cardboard, 21⅜ × 29⅜ inches. Collection of the Whitney Museum of American Art.

Below and facing page: William Grant Still was a prolific composer in every musical genre, including opera and ballet. Still has been one of the most performed Black composers.

Below: Associated with the premieres of the operas *Four Saints in Three Acts* and *Porgy and Bess* as choral director, Eva Jessye is a famed arranger of many spirituals and other works.

cago Ballet. Another piece of ballet music is *Sahdji*. Based on African subjects, it has a scenario by Bruce Nugent and Alain Locke and was first presented in Rochester, at the Eastman Conservatory.

Another of America's most famous composers, Duke Ellington, was a contemporary of Still. Ellington was also extremely prolific and enjoyed universal renown mainly because of his primacy in the world of jazz. While most of Ellington's work was designed for his own jazz ensemble – even more specifically for the virtuoso performers who made up his orchestra – he also composed for the symphony orchestra. His major suites, such as *Black, Brown and Beige* and *New World A-Coming*, are only heard at their best with full symphonic treatment. Ellington traveled widely and often based pieces on travel experiences, such as *The Far East Suite*. Many of his songs have become standards; a few, such as *Sophisticated Lady*, are among the best songs in the American musical repertory and are now included in many classic recitals. Ellington also collaborated with other composers, notably Billy Strayhorn. Among their joint compositions are *A Drum is A Woman* and *Virign Islands Suite*.

Two composers linked by their settings of Langston Hughes' poems are Margaret Bonds and Howard Swanson. An associate of Florence Price, Margaret Bonds composed the cantata *The Ballad of the Brown King* to a libretto by Hughes. She wrote many songs as well as larger works for orchestra. Swanson, who studied with Nadia Boulanger in Paris, had his *A Short Symphony* performed in 1950 by the New York Philharmonic. The works of both

Above: As a composer, arranger and stylist, Duke Ellington produced hundreds of pieces which captivated audiences. His larger-scale works attempted poetic expression of racial and historical themes as in *Black, Brown and Beige.*

these composers are often sung in recital today by such singers as Leontyne Price.

The roster of outstanding Black composers also includes Ulysses Kay, George Walker, T.J. Anderson, Hale Smith, David Baker, Undine Moore, Coleridge-Taylor Perkinson, Dorothy Rudd Moore, and Noel DaCosta.

Euro-Classical Performers

In the nineteenth century a number of Blacks achieved success as performers outside the Black tradition. They included the concert singer Elizabeth Taylor Greenfield, known as "the Black Swan," and the pianist "Blind Tom" Bethune. However, it was with the triumph of Roland Hayes in the 1920s that a succession of performing artists, principally singers, became stars. One of the most beloved was Marian Anderson, the possessor of an extraordinary contralto voice. Her artistry and near saintly temperament helped her to conquer recital halls worldwide, despite frequent humiliations because of racial prejudice. The most notorious of her rebuffs was the refusal by the Daughters of the American Revolution in 1939 to allow her to sing in Constitution Hall, then the main concert hall in the nation's capital. Eleanor Roosevelt resigned from the DAR in protest. The snub was turned into a triumph for Marian Anderson – and at least a momentary one for her country – when President Roosevelt's Secretary of the Interior, Harold Ickes, invited her to sing a public Easter concert in front of the Lincoln Memorial.

Marian Anderson reached her highest artistry in German *lieder*, particularly Schubert, opera arias, and spirituals but her opportunity to sing at America's leading opera house, the Metropolitan, came too late to allow her to solidify an operatic career. Two of her contemporaries had, however, looked toward careers in opera – both Lillian Evanti and Caterina Jarboro appeared in European opera houses and on secondary opera stages in the United States. In the thirties and early forties, George Gershwin's *Porgy and Bess* gave a number of dramatic singers their chance to sing opera. Among the fine portrayals of Bess were Anne Wiggins Brown, and Etta Moten. Todd Duncan was the most noteworthy Porgy. Duncan and Moten both enjoyed long recital careers – he also starred on Broadway in *Cabin in the Sky* and *Lost in the Stars*, and she occasionally did film work. A second opera of the thirties that gave Blacks a break in this field was Virgil Thomson's *Four Saints in Three Acts*.

Paul Robeson, internationally famous as actor and singer, was celebrated for his work in European opera houses, particularly in England and Russia. But he did not stick to opera, instead dazzling audiences in recitals between stage and film roles.

Other leading Black singers of the thirties and forties were Dorothy Maynor, a lyric soprano of great tonal purity; Ellabelle Davis, a dramatic soprano who appeared in opera in Mexico; and Carol Brice, a contralto whose intelligence and talent won her critical kudos as "the new Marian Anderson."

The creation of the New York City Opera in the 1940s opened opportunities for Blacks while the stage of the Metropolitan remained stubbornly closed to them. Todd Duncan, Camilla Williams, and

Below: Natalie Hinderas is one of the major concert pianists of the United States. At home throughout the repertory, she has played the works of Black composers in recitals throughout the world.

Below: One of the consummate vocal artists of the century, William Warfield has exhibited not only a capacity to master an extremely wide range of repertory with differing stylistic and vocal demands, but he is also a singing actor of tremendous talent, as indicated by his virtual identification with the character of Porgy and Bess.

Lawrence Winters were among the singers of the company in its early years. The first Black woman to have full company status at the Metropolitan is the coloratura soprano Mattiwilda Dobbs, who has also sung in the major opera houses of the world. Her concert career, with a repertory drawn from Spanish, French, Italian, German, Scandinavian, Brazilian, and American composers, has been truly exceptional.

The elegant revival of *Porgy and Bess* in 1953 was once more a gateway to opera for many singers, including Inez Matthews and Miriam Burton, and the production brought stardom for William Warfield and Leontyne Price. Warfield had already triumphed in recital, acclaimed for both vocal and interpretive artistry. He had had a minor role in the Marc Blitzstein opera *Regina* on Broadway in 1949, but with *Porgy and Bess*, he established himself as one of the world's leading singing actors. Leontyne Price reached the pinnacle of the Metropolitan in 1961 after a recital debut in 1954, appearances in television opera, and operatic success in Vienna and at La Scala, Milan. She was immediately accorded the status of prima donna. Price starred in the opera that inaugurated the Metropolitan's new house at Lincoln Center, Samuel Barber's *Anthony and Cleopatra*. Although the opera was not well received, she herself received the highest of praise.

Other Black women singers of international reputation in opera and recital are Martina Arroyo, Grace Bumbry, Shirley Verrett, and Jessye Norman. Black male singers have had greater difficulty in overcoming the deep-seated prejudice barring them but among the few who have

Facing page: Among jazz musicians, Art Tatum was universally acknowledged as a great piano virtuoso. His stylistic ingenuity is reflected in the existence of both studio and "live" recordings.

Below: Lionel Hampton and Billie Holiday perform at the Metropolitan Opera House during Esquire's Annual All-American Jazz Concert.

sung roles at the Metropolitan are George Shirley, Seth McCoy, and Simon Estes.

Black instrumentalists have also had limited access to the concert stage. For example, the pianist Hazel Harrison could not make the breakthrough in spite of a legendary bravura technique. After studying in Europe with Busoni and Petri, she was foiled at home when seeking a recital career and spent most of the thirties and forties as a teacher at Howard University. A more recent piano virtuosa, Natalie Hinderas, has had a more fulfilling career, but teaching has also been essential to her survival. Hinderas displays an impressive technique and has a large repertory. She played the premier of George Walker's piano concerto which was commissioned by the Atlanta Symphony.

Leon Bates, a pupil of Natalie Hinderas, has attained celebrity as a recital pianist, but the best-known and busiest Black pianist is Andre Watts, whose fame is worldwide. Other remarkable if less renowned pianists include Eugene Haynes, Robert Jordan, Raymond Jackson, and Frances Walker. The duo-piano team of Wilfred Delphin and Edwin Romain came to prominence in the seventies, while the eighties saw the return to the concert stage of the remarkable Armenta Rogers.

Among conductors making a name for themselves are Leonard de Paur, Everett Lee, James De Preist, and Henry Lewis. Dean Dixon, the most acclaimed of Black conductors, held major posts in both Germany and Australia but was never considered by an American orchestra. The great expectations held for Calvin Simmons, the young conductor of the Oakland Symphony,

Below: An accomplished singer, it was as a bandleader who lived and encouraged excellent instrumental talents that Cab Calloway made his greatest contribution to jazz. As a stage performer in revivals of *Porgy and Bess* and *Hello Dolly*, and as a film performer in *Stormy Weather* and other films, he had a great impact on his contemporaries.

Facing page: With her unerring natural pitch, a warm and appealing voice, and her straightforward reading of lyrics, Ella Fitzgerald has maintained herself before the jazz public for longer than any female singer. Her "scat" performances in the style of Louis Armstrong have also been esteemed.

were shattered by his accidental death by drowning.

Performers, composers, and conductors are the subject of Raoul Abdul's *Blacks in Classical Music*. Abdul, the music critic of the *Amsterdam News*, is himself a *lieder* singer and teacher of great merit.

Black Music: Blues, Jazz, Pop and Gospel

The stream of Black music is both wide and deep and resists the attempt of some commentators to isolate one current or the other by pronouncements about authenticity. From the perspective of the Trans-Urban Culture, we may distinguish four principal categories: blues, jazz, pop and gospel. All have their roots in an earlier period, and all were shaped in part by the record industry, which was the chief vehicle of their far-flung reach. The categories are not exclusive. They flow into and feed off one another. The practitioners too have moved from one category to the other without difficulty, and sometimes without even knowing it.

In general, Trans-Urban Black music is that created by Blacks primarily for Blacks. It continues the tradition of music-making for social occasions that goes back to the early nineteenth century. Here again, it is a two-way street. Much Black music is savored by white audiences, and many Black audiences enjoy music outside their tradition, such as opera, symphony, and country music. There have been top white practitioners in jazz and pop while Blacks have succeeded in almost every established musical style.

Three towering figures who preceded the Trans-Urban explosion of music on records are Will Marion

Facing page: Well-known gospel soloist, Sister Rosetta Tharpe.

Below: The greatest of the female jazz pianists, Mary Lou Williams was an important band arranger, and later a composer of music in larger forms for concert hall and for the church.

Cook, James Reese Europe, and W.C. Handy. Cook, a conservatory-trained musician who studied violin with Joachim in Berlin and composition with Dvorak in New York, was a pioneer figure in the early Black musicals of the 1890s. Building on developments in ragtime and jazz, he created a Syncopated Orchestra which performed in Europe and the United States in 1919, creating a sensation. Europe, who was also a violinist, was connected with the earlier Black musicals, too. In 1910 he formed the Clef Club Orchestra which performed concerts before World War I. During the war he was a bandmaster, and as such introduced Black music to France. Handy, originally a band musician in the Sousa tradition, was also composer, arranger, publisher, and impresario whose influence was felt for three decades after he published the first blues in 1912. In 1928 Handy gave a much-praised concert at Carnegie Hall in which he reviewed the history of written Black music.

Blues interweaves with jazz in the earliest recordings of the Trans-Urban Culture. In fact, the classic blues of Bessie Smith and Ma Rainey can be said to be a song made of jazz. Blues are both sad and joyous, and the great blues artists are concerned with musical effect as much as the lyrics. Such a concern is behind the creation of scat singing by Louis Armstrong, a style that hints at an instrumental technique with the voice. Armstrong inspired generations of Black musicians, not the least Billie Holiday who bore the crown of the great women blues singers of the thirties. Scat renditions were taken up by Cab Calloway and Ella Fitzgerald.

At least three women named Smith – Bessie, Clara, and Trixie – and none apparently related, belong to the roster of blues singers of the twenties. Ethel Waters, Alberta Hunter, and Blanche Calloway were better known as popular ballad singers, but they also sang blues songs on occasion.

Gospel music is closely allied to the blues and had a nearly parallel development being originally church music with roots in the hymns of the evangelical or "down-home" churches of the end of the nineteenth century. The Reverend Charles A. Tindley, a Methodist pastor of Philadelphia, is credited as the first composer of gospel hymns – he worked at the beginning of the twentieth century. Gospel music is a Folk-Urban art form that sprang up among the less formal church congregations, existing side by side with the standard hymns.

Gospel music was transformed in the Trans-Urban Culture, taking on elements of style and performance from both blues and jazz. This transformation, which probably went on in a number of places at the same time, is most closely linked with Chicago and the work of Thomas A. Dorsey. As a jazz musician, Dorsey had been a member of Ma Rainey's instrumental ensemble. His gospel career began in the late twenties and by only a few years later, gospel groups and choirs had burst forth throughout Black America, and were already moving out of the churches to be enjoyed by people as entertainment.

Among the well-known gospel soloists and groups are Roberta Martin and the Martin Singers, Clara Ward and the Ward Sisters, Sister Rosetta Tharpe and the greatly admired Mahalia Jackson who was

Below: An articulate spokesman for his own achievement, Jelly Roll Morton could lay valid claim to the development of a distinctive role as pianist and group leader in the formative pre-recorded years of early jazz.

acclaimed as the greatest of them all. Jackson, a native of New Orleans, was influenced by Bessie Smith, whom she heard on records. Among male gospel performers of note are Brother John Sellers, a protégé of Mahalia Jackson, James Cleveland, founder of the annual Gospel Workshop and Andrae Crouch. A host of popular singers come from the gospel tradition, including Aretha Franklin and Della Reese.

Perhaps the most important transitional figure of the jazz world of the twenties was Jelly Roll Morton, pianist and composer. His career began in New Orleans, the cradle of jazz, around 1902, and his path crossed most of the early figures in jazz and blues. Jelly Roll began recording with groups in Chicago in 1923, and in New York in 1928. Recognizing his pivotal role and extensive knowledge, the library of Congress made a series of records with Jelly Roll in 1938 on which he interspersed comment with solo pieces. A similar series of recordings with him backed by a group were done in New York in 1939 and 1940. Jelly Roll's personal claims were extravagant, but his artistic achievement could hardly be exaggerated.

The two titans of jazz in the twenties were Louis Armstrong and Duke Ellington, both adored in their day and after. Armstrong's virtuosity and creativity and trumpeter were crucial to the development of jazz, since he provided a model and set standards both for groups and soloists. Armstrong joined other musicians from New Orleans in Chicago in 1922 and played there off and on until he went to New York in 1924, alternating between the two cities for the rest of the twenties. Ellington came to New York from Washington in 1922.

Previous pages and above: The single most important innovator and creative talent in jazz performance, Louis Armstrong, as trumpet-player and vocalist, was idolized by the Black public in the early years of his career.

A good pianist himself, he also developed a very distinctive style of ensemble playing, building an orchestra in which every individual was worthy of soloist stature. His creativity as a composer was a particularly fruitful one. Ellington was associated with the Cotton Club revues in his early career.

By the mid-1920s Fletcher Henderson started the trend toward big bands. Henderson's reed player from 1921 to 1926 was Don Redman. Both were well-trained musicians in the Euro-Classical tradition – Redman's arrangement of *The Stampede* in 1926 for the Henderson orchestra fairly well sets the pattern later developed by Henderson as his own arranger and leader. It was to be the frame used by arrangers for the big bands of the thirties, all of whom followed Henderson's lead except Ellington, whose own style was individual and inimitable.

Many of the outstanding instrumentalists and vocalists led bands at one time or another. These included the pianists Earl "Fatha" Hines and Fats Waller, and the singers Cab Calloway and Billy Eckstine. Count Basie and Jimmy Lunceford scored high as band leaders. Count Basie, who had a long and durable career, was the chief representative of Kansas City jazz, the successor to the pioneer of that school, Bennie Moten. Lunceford's orchestra, which seldom gave over to virtuoso performance, set a high standard of ensemble work for the jazz world.

One of the most honored of the jazz world's greats was Sidney Bechet, whose instruments were the clarinet and the soprano saxophone. Bechet went to Europe in 1919 with Will Marion Cook's Syncopated Orchestra. There his playing became

Facing page: The most enduring popular family singing group, the Mills Brothers were headlines in Vaudeville in the early 1930s. Their influence was wide and they captured the affections of a loyal public.

Previous pages: One of the greatest band leaders of the big-band era, Count Basie forged a highly individual swinging style, which was much imitated by his peers.

Below: Billie Holiday, a blues singer of unsurpassed talent.

the subject of the first musicological study of jazz, an article published by Ernest Ansermet in *La Revue Romane*. Bechet spent most of his life in Europe, dying there in 1959. The tenor saxophonist Coleman Hawkins also spent a good deal of time in Europe in the thirties – his 1939 recording of *Body and Soul* is one of the classics of jazz. Hawkins survived the bebop era with his individual style intact. Lester Young, who played tenor saxophone and clarinet, was one of the most influential jazz figures of the thirties, forties, and fifties, remaining so to the end of his life in 1959.

The trumpet, clarinet, saxophone, and piano are the most common instruments of jazz, but Lionel Hampton entered the ranks of the great jazz musicians playing the vibraphone. A flamboyant soloist, he also became a major band leader.

The list of the great jazz pianist begins with Jelly Roll Morton and goes on quickly to James P. Johnson. A peerless performer in the ragtime tradition, Johnson backed such famous blues and jazz singers as Bessie Smith and Ethel Waters. He had a big influence on the new York school of pianists including Fats Waller and Art Tatum, two other giants of the keyboard. Waller was a major songwriter and organist as well. His enduring compositions include *Ain't Misbehavin'* and *Honeysuckle Rose*. Tatum, who was blind, had studied violin as well as piano. He usually played solo and demonstrated a technical perfection that was legendary. Two younger pianists who marked the history of jazz beginning in the thirties were Teddy Wilson and Mary Lou Williams. Wilson became best known for his performances with the Benny

Goodman trio. He taught jazz piano in New York conservatories and was highly esteemed for his musical technique. Mary Lou Williams was soloist and arranger for Andy Kirk and His Clouds of Joy, creating the style of that orchestra. After leaving the Kirk orchestra, she went on to perform with small groups or as a soloist and also composed extensively in larger musical forms. More than any other jazz pianist, she moved with the newest currents throughout her career.

There were many important jazz singers in the thirties. Unique among them is the durable Mills Brothers quartet, whose fame lasted for decades. They were not very sophisticated musically, and much of their material was embarrassingly sentimental, but they captured the public affection. The greatest singer to emerge in the thirties was Billie Holiday. After recording with Benny Goodman in 1933 and other orchestras for another six years, she went solo in 1939 – the year she made her epochal recording of *Strange Fruit*.

The most popular of the Black jazz male vocalists in the thirties was Billy Eckstine, who led his own orchestra in the forties. His recording of the Johnson Hubert tune *I'm Falling for You*, with the Earl Hines orchestra, is one of his best known.

In the thirties, too, Ella Fitzgerald began her journey to world fame with the Chick Webb orchestra and, from the mid-forties on, was sought after as a guest artist by jazz groups, bands, and even symphony orchestras. She recorded with the Mills Brothers and Louis Armstrong and made big-selling solo recordings of ballads by Cole Porter and George Gershwin. Singers who came shortly after the thirties, but whose careers followed the mold of thirties jazz singers included Sarah Vaughan, Carmen McRae, and Al Hibbler.

The career of Lena Horne is a special one. Beginning as a singer and dancer in the Cotton Club, she later sang with the orchestras of Cab Calloway and Noble Sissle. Then she made a breakthrough as the first Black singer to appear with a white orchestra, that of Charlie Barnet. She had a success in films, followed by years of always being in demand for top nightclub spots. Her long career was capped by her own one-person show on Broadway in the 1980s, *Lena, the Lady and Her Music.*

Mabel Mercer was another singer with a special history. In 1925 she replaced Florence Mills in the production *Dover to Dixie,* her first acquaintance with Black American music. She came to New York from Paris where she had been working at the nightclub run by the Black American blues singer Ada "Bricktop" Smith. Mercer was a singer's singer, much esteemed as an interpreter of the popular song by Billie Holiday and numerous others. While she never achieved great personal fame or wealth, she deeply influenced many later popular idols such as Frank Sinatra and Johnny Mathis.

Nat King Cole was one of the first of the ballad singers to accompany himself on the piano as he sang. Cole was a first-rate jazz pianist, influenced by Earl "Fatha" Hines and Teddy Wilson but with an individuality of his own. His early success as a nightclub vocalist led him to concentrate on singing, putting piano playing into the background, a choice that led him to become the leading romantic ballad singer of the 1950s. He also made a breakthrough in the relatively new medium of tele-

Below: The most honoured of gospel singers, Mahalia Jackson lived successively in two great centers of Black music, New Orleans and Chicago. Though her style was akin to the blues, she publicly sang only gospel and inspirational songs.

Above: Beginning as a teenage singer and dancer at the Cotton Club, Lena Horne's development into an actress and singer in films and on stage was crowned by a long-running revue in the 1980s.

Below: Nat King Cole was one of the first of the ballad singers to accompany himself on the piano.

Facing page: Ray Charles' style and virtuosity made him an extremely popular and well-recorded performer.

vision, hosting his own series toward the end of the decade.

The next male singer-pianist in line to Nat King Cole is Ray Charles. Like Cole, he started with his own trio. His Southern roots made him cling to the blues tradition, away from the romantic style of Cole, and his success has remained based on his singing of bluesy songs. Two Black women, Nina Simone and Roberta Flack, are singer-pianists of outstanding talent. They both lean heavily on the blues-jazz tradition in their song interpretations but both also have great skill in "recomposing," as in Simone's *Porgy* and Flack's *Killing Me Softly*.

The period of the thirties is called the Swing era, a time when big bands held sway. Big bands continued to be greatly popular in the forties, but they were more commercial in nature after 1940. Innovations, left to small ensembles, gave rise to bebop or bop and this jazz style brought about a fundamental change in the relation of musicians and audiences. Until the end of the Swing era, jazz had genuinely been the music of the people, a music still to be danced to. Bebop created a diversion – it was "serious" jazz, demanding quiet and attentive audiences. The new players became distanced from the jazz tradition, often seeming to play for themselves in a jam session to which the public was grudgingly admitted.

Common consent has conferred the designation of King and Queen of Soul on James Brown and Aretha Franklin. Both of them owe much to the tradition of gospel music, even to the preachiness of some of their lyrics. Brown usually works with his own groups, putting on a show like a stage production.

Two singers who started in the fif-

ties stand apart from the jazz-blues-gospel lineage: Harry Belafonte and Johnny Mathis. Belafonte shot to stardom with his very personal renditions of Jamaican and other Caribbean folksongs, although one of the most famous, *Yellowbird*, is not a Jamaican folksong at all but a composed Haitian piece, *Choucoune.* The voice of Johnny Mathis – soft, sweet, and romantic – made him the heir of Nat King Cole as one of the world's most popular balladeers. His art shows the influence of Mabel Mercer and Latin romantic singers.

Bebop, that great divide between serious and popular jazz, began in the early forties at Minton's, a club in Harlem. Musicians exploring new rhythmic, melodic, and harmonic ideas gave full sway to improvisation, which had always been basic to the development of jazz. The style spread as performers moved from Minton's to other clubs, and as the number of bebop adherents increased.

Two primary figures in bebop were Charlie Parker and Dizzy Gillespie. Parker, an alto saxophonist from Kansas City, played in a number of big bands including those of Noble Sissle and Billy Eckstine. By 1945 he and trumpeter Gillespie, playing in a quintet at Minton's, had ushered in a new, fully developed jazz style. Gillespie also formed and led a big band. Unlike other serious jazz figures of the post-1940 era, he periodically returned to band-leading, fostering the talents of a number of outstanding musicians in that role.

The regular pianist at the Harlem club was Thelonious Monk, the third great of the bebop school. Others of note are Kenny Clarke, drummer, and Charlie Christian, guitarist. Two other drummers early on the bebop scene are Art Blakey and Max Roach,

Both Nina Simone (below) and Roberta Flack (facing page) took blues to wider audiences in the 1970s.

Facing page: Acclaimed the "Queen of Soul", Aretha Franklin, like many other singers, has imparted a gospel sound to most of her musical performances.

Left: In bringing Jamaican and other Caribbean folk songs to a wide public, Harry Belafonte carved out a distinctive niche in American culture for himself as singer and interpreter. He has been an important patron of a number of other artistic talents.

who since have been the most creative musicians in percussion.

By the late forties the bebop style had drawn to it the young trumpeter Miles Davis, destined to become the most influential figure in jazz for several decades. Davis was at the source of one of the two major currents of the fifties, cool jazz. Another leader of the cool jazz trend, pianist John Lewis, founder of the Modern Jazz Quartet, with Davis had impact on the music world beyond jazz.

The bebop of the forties became the hard bop of the fifties, a style dominated by Roach and Blakey. Other bop innovators of the fifties included Donald Byrd, trumpet, Sonny Rollins, tenor saxophone, and Charlie Mingus, bass and piano.

Serious jazz of the fifties was strongly marked by racial integration among players, innovators, and theorists of the music, an integration kept healthy by the Newport Jazz Festival, inaugurated in the summer of 1954. A charismatic figure of the fifties jazz was tenor saxophonist John Coltrane, who had played in Dizzy Gillespie's big band. Coltrane was with Miles Davis from 1955 to 1960, after which he led his own quartet. The sixties have been called the period of free jazz and Coltrane's position in it is crucial. However, the alto saxophonist, Ornette Coleman, became the undisputed king of free jazz. He drew on theoretical studies in music, translating them into unconventional use. He also played the violin and trumpet.

No study of serious jazz could exclude Archie Shepp, tenor saxophonist, and Cecil Taylor and Billy Taylor, pianists. Billy Taylor has emerged as the informal historian of jazz, much in the manner of Duke Ellington. Playing, composing, and

Below: Johnny Mathis continued in the tradition of Cole.

Facing page: The most extroverted of the group of musicians among whom bebop arose in the early 1940s, Dizzy Gillespie exhibited a gift both for stylistic innovation and for communication with a large public.

lecturing, he has been a link between serious jazz and the public, a much-needed link because, after the fifties, serious jazz went its own way – often too calculated or too political for public taste.

Miles Davis managed to join the new electronic sounds of the sixties with serious jazz. His "electric jazz" won him a larger and more youthful audience, keeping him in the lead on the jazz scene.

One of the outstanding pop stars who shows a feeling for the jazz tradition is Stevie Wonder, a performer since childhood. Both singer and songwriter, his inventiveness appeals both to admirers of Coltrane and Davis as well as to the broad international pop world.

Left: Stevie Wonder's influence and talent have led to many recordings, and to much flattering imitation of his style.

Below: Frequently compared with Louis Armstrong because of the largeness of his talent and the weight of his influence, Miles Davis is ultimately a very introspective creator whose direct communication with a larger public often comes with great difficulty.

Facing page: Michael Jackson, first as a member of the Jackson Five and then as a solo performer, has won an international following.

Blacks in Dance

The social dances of Black America hark back to the vitality and intensity of African dance. These dances, beginning with the hoedown of the Folk-Rural Culture, left behind any ceremonial significance and are fundamentally for fun. They have drawn in particular on two sources: African body movement and Euro-American floor patterns.

The Folk-Rural population often imitated the dances of "white folks" when they were out of sight of their bosses. Later, on the stage, black-faced minstrels popularized a kind of eccentric dance that made fun of Blacks. What they didn't know was that they were ridiculing Blacks ridiculing whites – they simply thought that Blacks were too ungraceful to execute the movements of European dances.

From the 1890s on, Black stage dancing constantly led the way in musical comedy and vaudeville. The great Bill Robinson and many other Black dancers were headliners in vaudeville, the most popular theater entertainment in the United States before the coming of sound movies.

The opening of *Shuffle Along* on Broadway in 1921 revolutionized stage dancing and the specialties of its soloists and chorus line were rapidly imitated by white shows. Whites, in fact, felt threatened by the popularity and success of the Black musicals. A song in the 1922 Ziegfeld Follies expressed this feeling when it said that "It's Getting Dark on Old Broadway." It was not long before it got lighter as whites forced the Blacks off Broadway and absorbed their material.

In 1924 Black musicals were still around, and Black dancers starred behind the footlights. In that year *Chocolate Dandies* featured Josephine Baker and Charlie Davis. The precision chorus work of this show started a second wave of imitation which reached its peak in the Rockettes of Radio City and the dancing routines of Busby Berkeley in Hollywood films. Bill "*Bojangles*" Robinson, who became known as the King of Tap Dancers, made his Broadway splash in *Black-birds* of 1928, which also features "*Snake Hips*" Tucker. Robinson was already 50 years old, but went on to have a long career on stage and in films. Tucker was an unequalled eccentric dancer, better known as a nightclub performer – he appeared for long runs at the Cotton Club, dancing to the music of the Duke Ellington orchestra. The unlettered Tucker had no successful imitators of his specialty – a masculine version of the shimmy, which was traditionally reserved for female dancers. Both Josephine Baker and Ethel Waters were really outstanding shimmy dancers.

Tap dancing was a mainstay of American entertainment from the days of the vaudeville circuit to Broadway revues, to screen musicals until their virtual disappearance in the fifties. Though there was a revival of live tap dancing in the seventies, this dance form is known largely through the rerunning of old films on television. Both film and Broadway gave only a little exposure to the Black tap tradition. The Hoofer's Club in Harlem, run by Lonnie Hicks, was for several decades a combination rehearsal-instruction-social center for Black tap dancers.

Among the outstanding Black tap dancers was the legendary King "*Rastus*" Brown, who charged Bill Robinson with excessive borrowing.

Facing page: Grande dame of the rockers, Tina Turner forged a new career in the 1980s.

Below: "King of Tap Dancers," Bill Robinson achieved Broadway celebrity in his forties and went on to become an important figure in films of the 1930s.

A slightly younger contemporary was Ulysses "*Kid*" Thompson, an extremely acrobatic dancer. He inspired many of the leading white tap dancers for whom the Robinson style was too "Black." John Bubbles was also a fine tapper. His surprising talent as a singer earned him the role of Sporting Life in *Porgy and Bess*, though it was intended for an operatic voice. Of the elegant team of Coles and Atkins, Charles "*Honi*" Coles lived to reap wild praise in the seventies' revival of stage tap shows.

A Black social dance of close bodily contact, called the slowdrag, was danced on the Broadway stage in the 1929 production of *Harlem* as part of a rent party scene. A little too smoldering for most theatergoers of the time, it was denounced by some as indecent.

Clifton Webb in 1929 performed a dance called "*High Yaller*" in the "*Moanin' Low*" episode of *The Little Show*. It was a kind of adaptation of Snake Hips Tucker's shimmy-like movement. Its traces can still be seen in the "viper" movements of the ballet *Slaughter on Tenth Avenue* choreographed by George Balanchine for the musical *On Your Toes* in 1936. Webb's dance was choreographed by *Buddy Bradley*, a leading Black dancer, teacher, and coach of white Broadway stars, who listed among his pupils Mae West, Gilda Gray, Ruby Keeler, Fred and Adele Astaire, Eleanor Powell, Lucille Ball, and Paul Draper. Bradley never got a crack at the big Broadway shows, and left the United States for England in 1933. There he gained the fame his talent deserved.

No Black officially choreographed a Broadway show before the coming of Katherine Dunham with her own dance reviews. In fact, however,

white dance directors always allowed Black performers to find their own way within the larger patterns blocked out for the shows – Balanchine followed this open policy in *Cabin in the Sky* (1940), for instance, and Eugene Loring in *Carmen Jones* (1943). Only after 1960 did Black choreographers win Broadway assignments, and then for white controlled shows with all or predominantly Black casts.

The most important Black choreographeres on Broadway are Talley Beatty, Donald McKayle, Louis Johnson, Geoffrey Holder, George Faison, and Billy Wilson. Among Black choreographers for the opera stage are Dunham, Johnson, Alvin Ailey, and Arthur Mitchell. All of these made a name for themselves as dancers first, and all have worked with dance companies concerned with pure dance.

Edna Guy was the first Black dancer involved in the modern dance movement. She admired the pioneering Denishawn company, some of whose dance tableaux had a kinship with the amateur pageants then popular in Black Trans-Urban Culture. She organized a dance group in Harlem in the early 1930s, in which she performed some of Ruth St Denis's own solos.

The two most important figures on New York's Black dance scene in the early thirties were Helmesley Winfield and Asadata Dafora. Winfield, encouraged by the leading lights of the white modern dance movement, organized the Negro Art Dance Company. In 1933 this company performed the dance scenes in the opera, *The Emperor Jones*, at the Metropolitan. Winfield died at the age of 26, leaving the dance world the poorer.

Asadata Dafora was born in Sierra

Facing page: Bringing insights from anthropology into her study of Black dance in the Caribbean and in the United States, Katherine Dunham forged a theatrical mode that inspired imitation throughout the world.

Above: As the first Black dancer to become a principal in an American ballet company, Arthur Mitchell appeared in many roles in ballets created by George Balanchine for the New York City Ballet, including *Agon, Bugaku,* and *A Midsummer Night's Dream.*

Leone and came to Harlem in 1929. Five years later he presented his dance drama, *Kykunkor,* to small but enthusiastic audiences in New York. His second work, *Zungura,* opened in 1938. Dafora spent the rest of his life eking out a living as a concert dancer, unable to make the big breakthrough he had hoped for in dance.

The single most important figure in the whole of Black American dance history was Katherine Dunham, who began her career in Chicago in the early thirties as dancer, teacher, and choreographer. In 1940 Dunham appeared on Broadway with members of her troupe in *Cabin in the Sky,* with choreography by Balanchine. In fact, much of the choreography was hers and had been performed previously to smaller audiences. Dunham choreographed several complete shows for her company, playing Broadway and then touring worldwide for many years. An anthropologist by education, she studied at the University of Chicago and did extensive fieldwork in Haiti and Jamaica. She drew on these studies for inspiration in her choreography and, in so doing, preserved many traditional dances of the Caribbean, Latin America, and her own country. Dunham established a dance school in New York and included Black culture studies in the curriculum. Students of the Dunham school won places in many of the country's dance companies.

Beginning in the late forties as a soloist and small company artist, Pearl Primus enjoyed a spectacular reputation in modern dance. Primus began to specialize in African dance early in her career and, with her husband Percival Borde, made field trips to Africa to feed and reinforce her art. The public taste for African dance in the United States was fueled by the visits of African companies such as the *Ballets Africains* of Guinea. African companies based in the United States include those of Dinizulu, Chuck Davis, and Arthur Hall. Charles Moore, once a Dunham dancer, heads a company that features African dance, while also keeping works from the repertoires of Dunham and Dafora before new dance audiences.

Alvin Ailey and his American Dance Theater became the most widely known and influential of all American dance groups in the 1980s. Ailey, himself a dancer trained in the Lester Horton dance company and studios in California, came to New York in the mid-fifties. His talents as a choreographer and artistic director were quickly recognized, and his work generated mass excitement and critical acclaim. Ailey's company was racially mixed but predominantly Black. By the late seventies the Ailey complex included the principal company, a repertory company, a workshop company, and a large-scale professional school.

Ailey had an international reputation and some of his ballets are still danced by companies from Israel to Venezuela. However, most of his work was intended for the American Dance Theater and their performances of work like *Revelations* and *Blues Suite* never failed to electrify audiences. Both the Paris Ballet and the National Ballet of Cuba turned to Ailey for choreography and, in turn, he sought and welcomed into his own company's repertory, work by most of the leading choreographers of the day, including Dunham, Primus, Beatty, Johnson, McKayle, Faison, Diane McIntyre, Billy Williams, Eleo Pomare, and Bill T. Jones. Most

of these artists have had their own companies at one time or other, usually as a showpiece for their own particular work. The most dynamic choreographer to emerge from the ranks of the Ailey company has been Ulysses Dove. Two outstanding and diverse choreographers whose works are associated with their own companies are Gus Solomans Jr. and Garth Fagan.

While some Blacks wanted careers in classical ballet, they mostly regarded this field as closed to them. Nevertheless there were excellent Black ballet teachers as early as the 1930s, notably Essie Marie Dorsey in Philadelphia, and there were enough Black ballet-trained dancers to encourage the creation of all-Black ballet troupes. The first notable one was the Von Grona Company. In the fifties, Doris Jones and Claire Haywood established the Capital Ballet in Washington and performed a brief season annually. Capital Ballet pro-

Below: Honored dancer, choreographer and teacher, Dr Pearl Primus has been hailed as a prophet of the Trans-African epoch.

Right: The Alvin American Dance Theater is the best-known American dance company worldwide and has appeared in dozens of countries around the world. Alvin Ailey, a great choreographer in his own right, generously invites the work of other choreographers into his repertory, and fosters the choreographic talents of company members.

Below: The most famous of the many dancers associated with the Ailey Company, Judith Jamison is particularly known for her dramatic intensity, as expressed in such a work as *Cry*, created by Ailey for her. Jamison succeeded her mentor as artistic director of the Alvin Ailey American Dance Theater.

ductions were the equal or better of any regional ballet of the day.

The first Black ballet dancers to break into mainstream companies were Janet Collins and Arthur Mitchell. She was selected as the leading dancer of the Metropolitan Opera in 1951, and he made the New York City Ballet in 1956.

In the late sixties Arthur Mitchell started the teaching and organizing activities that ended in the formation of the Dance Theater of Harlem, which performs classic ballets, Balanchine works, and spectacular contemporary works.

The visits of two Caribbean dance companies had an influence on the significance for Black Americans. The Jamaican National Dance Theater Company has performed in New York, Atlanta, Miami, Houston, and other American cities and is directed by Rex Nettleford, a dancer-choreographer as well as a distinguished scholar. The National Ballet of Cuba, seen only in New York and Washington so far, is now directed by Alicia Alonso, once the prima of an American company.

A list of noteworthy Black dancers is incomplete without the following:

Carmen de Lavallade, dancer with Alvin Ailey and others.

Mary Hinkson, dancer with Martha Graham.

Matt Turney, dancer with Martha Graham.

Dudley Williams, dancer with Martha Graham and Alvin Ailey.

Sara Yarborough, dancer with Alvin Ailey and others, daughter and pupil of Lavinia Williams.

Donna Wood, dancer with Alvin Ailey.

Mel Tomlinson, dancer with Dance Theater of Harlem, Alvin Ailey, New York City Ballet.

Blacks in Sports

Blacks have won adulation as athletes in proportion to their admission to various fields of sport. The two earliest sports open to them were boxing and horse-racing, neither of which involved teamwork.

The first famous Black boxer was Tom Molyneux, a slave who was freed because of his skill. He later fought in England. There were other outstanding Black boxers through the years but the flamboyant and powerful Jack Johnson, heavyweight champion of the world from 1903 to 1915, placed Blacks in the forefront of American consciousness. Johnson's power and personality so traumatized white Americans that a call went out for a "white hope" to put him – and symbolically all Blacks – in line. Johnson remained self-confident and unhumbled throughout his life.

The next Black world heavyweight champion was Joe Louis, who held the title from 1937 to 1949. Louis' modest demeanour, tongue-tied

Below: Born a slave in Virginia, Tom Molyneux was one of the first well-known American boxers and fought in New York and in London, being matched there in a "battle-of-the-century" with pugilist Tom Cribb on 28th September, 1811.

Above: Pugnacious and arrogant in real life, a master of pugilism in the fight ring, heavyweight Jack Johnson was persecuted out of racial hatred by Americans who dreamed of a "white hope" to defeat him in the ring.

Facing page: The most highly respected boxer of his time, Joe Louis' prowess in the ring was complemented by a reserved and reticent public manner. Here he wins a knockout in the fourth round against Max Baer.

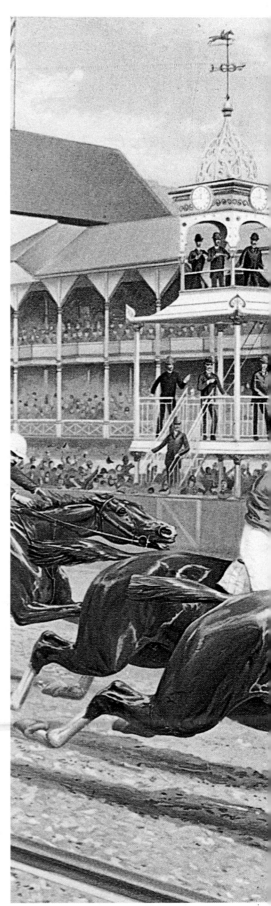

speech, and gentle nobility of character aroused less acrimony in whites, though the white hope syndrome persisted. Blacks held the world championship in an unbroken line from 1949 to the late seventies through Ezzard Charles, "Jersey Joe" Walcott, Floyd Patterson, Sonny Liston, Muhammad Ali, Joe Frazier, and George Foreman. In spite of this reality, the long-running comic strip of "Joe Palooka" presented a white man as the heavyweight title holder.

Muhammad Ali ranks with Johnson and Louis as the third all-time great. While experts rated him below Johnson and Louis in the ring, he was nevertheless vastly superior to any opponent he faced in his prime. His combination of great physical charm and scintillating verbal wit, including a facility for phrase-making and rhyming, widened his admiring public beyond ring enthusiasts. His popularity among white Americans decreased when he converted to the Nation of Islam, perceived as a hate group, and when he refused to serve in the army because of his opposition to the Vietnam War. For a while he was vilified almost as much as Johnson had been, but his later vindication in the courts and changes in the image of his religious affiliation brought him back into popular favor.

Black boxers have also excelled in other divisions of the ring. Henry Armstrong had the unique distinction of winning the featherweight, lightweight, and welterweight titles in 1937 and 1938. The solid Armstrong rival for public affection was the elegant and sartorial Sugar Ray Robinson, welterweight champion from 1947 to 1951 and middleweight champion twice in the fifties. Archie Moore, light-heavyweight champion

Previous pages, left: Sugar Ray Robinson in a characteristic pose.

Previous pages, right: Few sports figures have attained the worldwide celebrity of Muhammad Ali, whose verbal facility and quick wit made him a media figure. He survived a period of persecution for his anti-Vietnam War views and then returned to public favor.

Right: Black jockeys dominated the racing scene in the nineteenth century. This engraving depicts the *First Futurity* race, 1888, at Sheepshead Bay, by Louis Maurer.

Facing page, far right: Floyd Patterson, heavyweight champion, writing his memoirs.

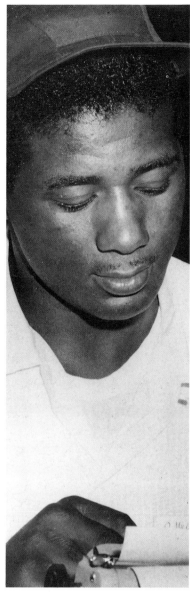

from 1953 to 1961, was another hero of the ring.

Black jockeys dominated horse-racing in the nineteenth century, both before and after emancipation. At the first Kentucky Derby in history, 14 of the 15 starting jockeys were black. Among the most famous riders was Isaac Murphy, who won three Derbies in the 1880s. The last Black jockey to ride in the Derby did so in 1911, after which a gradual policy of excluding them from racing finally succeeded. A slow return to the racing track has since occurred in the seventies.

Blacks have been tops in track and field sports since shortly after the Olympic games were revived in 1896. The most famous field athlete was Jesse Owens, whose amazing broad jump record of 1935 was unequalled for 30 years. Owens won gold medals in the broad jump and in two sprint categories at the Berlin Olympics of 1936, even though the Nazis tried to humiliate him as a non-Aryan. The continuing high standards of the United States team in international track and field events is due almost wholly to Black athletes and this is especially true of the broad jump, sprints, middle distance races, high jump, and hurdles. Carl Lewis and Ed Moses are the best-known record-breaking athletes of the 1980s.

Blacks were excluded from professional baseball until Jackie Robinson became a member of the Brooklyn Dodgers in 1947, after spending a year in the minor leagues in Montreal. Robinson overcame the hostility of his team mates, opposing teams, and public to become a respected athlete and well-liked man.

In 1948 the Cleveland Indians hired the legendary pitcher of the Negro Leagues, Satchel Paige. The

Above: After a brief career in the Negro leagues, Jackie Robinson was summoned to be the first openly acknowledged Black player in major league baseball. He survived hostility and insult, and ultimately earned wide respect in the sport.

Negro Leagues had come into exist-ence early in the century and played extended seasons for the Black public. They had been preceded by teams attached to hotels, traveling shows, and other businesses large enough to provide personnel for teams. During the thirties, members of the major Black dance bands fre-quently doubled as members of base-ball teams that played other band teams for recreation.

Though Satchel Paige was no longer in his prime when he entered the major leagues, he still made a great impact. As late as 1968 he was on the Atlanta Braves team, though he was not called upon to play. Other Black baseball players, who are either honored in the Baseball Hall of Fame or candidates for it, include Roy Campanella, Don Newcombe, Bob Gibson, Willie Mays, and Henry "*Hank*" Aaron, who set a new home-run record.

Football and basketball, the major college team sports, accepted Black players fairly early, though they had to wait to enter the ranks of the pro-fessionals. By the 1980s the Black presence in college and professional football was unmistakable, and was dominant in both college and profes-sional basketball.

Among the most outstanding of the earlier college football players were all-Americans Paul Robeson of Rutgers and Cornell's Jerome "*Brud*" Holland, later president of Hampton Institute, the United States Ambassador to Sweden, and a direc-tor of the New York Stock Exchange. The Heisman Trophy, college foot-ball's highest award, has gone chiefly to Black players since the early seventies, rousing the white hope syndrome in football. Among the top professional football players of the

Left: A basketball icon of both young and old, Earvin "Magic" Johnson, Jr., focused a new spotlight on the AIDS epidemic by public acknowl-edgement of his own infection.

Above: A major figure on the football field, O. J. Simpson has undertaken allied activities such as sports anouncing. His media status has been enhanced by his appearances in television commer-cials and print advertising.

Facing page: The track and field accomplishments of Jesse Owens at the Berlin Olympic Games in 1936 were considered by Black and white Americans alike as a symbolic victory over the Nazi doctrines of racial superiority proclaimed by Hitler.

Right: Wilma Rudolph's field and track accomplishments in the Rome Olympics of 1960, both as an individual and as a member of a relay team, gave her an unmatched worldwide celebrity.

eighties, all of whom gained college fame first, are Roosevelt Grier, Franco Harris, and O.J. Simpson.

The superstars among basketball players were Wilt Chamberlain, Walt Frazier, Bill Russell, Kareem Abdul-Jabbar, and Julius Erving. The Harlem Globetrotters earned a special niche with their clowning antics that did nothing to detract from their skill. When they began in 1927, this was the only professional team open to Black players. The Globetrotters have since become world famous, even to being the subject of a children's animated cartoon.

The three main spectator sports are a focus of American culture from the White House to the ghetto. While they have been a source of social and economic status for Black players and pride for Black spectators, their control and management have rested almost entirely in the hands of whites. There is only the occasional Black coach here, and manager there, although that is slowly changing.

The admission of Blacks to sports that often require country club membership, such as tennis, golf, and swimming has been grudging. Moreover, Blacks are not generally of the elite to whom these sports are natural. Arthur Ashe, however, conquered the tennis world as a member, and later captain, of the Davis cup team and winner of the singles title at Wimbledon. In golf, Lee Elder and Calvin Poole were successful and Althea Gibson, the finest of the Black women tennis players, attempted a career on the golf links after she left the courts.

Left: The first Black woman tennis star since the pioneering Althea Gibson, Zena Garrison competed at Wimbledon in 1991.

Pages 174–5: Ed
Moses takes a first in
the 400 metres
hurdles.

Previous pages, left:
Carl Lewis has been
one of the most
acclaimed track and
field stars of the
century.

Previous pages,
right: Combining
acrobatics, clowning
and serious play, the
Harlem Globetrot-
ters were, for a long
time, the only pro-
fessional outlet for
Black basketball
players.

Left: Sprinter
Evelyn Ashford won
a gold medal for the
sprint relay.

Right: Athlete
Florence Griffiths-
Joyner at the
Olympics.

CHAPTER IV

THE AFRICAN
AMERICAN AGE

Facing page: An articulate and analytical personality, Arthur Ashe reached the highest rank as a tennis player and maintained his position in public esteem by his subsequent activities in sports and education. His passing in 1993 was greatly mourned.

Below: The first Black Congressman from Mississippi since Reconstruction, Mike Espy was named Secretary of Agriculture in the Clinton administration – another first.

By the late eighties it was eminently clear that Black American culture had entered a new epoch, that of the Trans-African, a term made current first in respect to visual art by Jeff Donaldson and A.B. Spellman. The self-referencing term African-American, introduced on the initiative of scholar-activist Ramona Edelin and certified by Jesse Jackson from the visibility earned in his presidental campaigns, was accepted passionately by a large and vocal segment of the Black community.

The Trans-African epoch has roots stretching as far back as the early nineteenth century and may be fully appreciated only in connection with such concepts as Pan Africanism, African Diaspora, and Negritude. It is clear, however, that the epoch was directly initiated by the Black Power Movement, which challenged the integrationist ethos of the Civil Rights Movement of the sixties.

From the perspective of the nineties it is possible to recognize that mandated racism in the United States, having the sanction of law or rigidified custom, was brought to an end by the Civil Rights Movement, but that institutional racism, imbedded in attitude and consensus, has slowly yielded its grip and periodically resurges.

In the nineties, the general economic malaise in the United States, and generally in the West, bodes ill for the attempts of Blacks to gain access to resources and to overcome the dysfunctionalities that inflict what many have found it convenient to label the underclass.

Rising unemployment, inaccessible housing, and focused assault through the abandonment of social programs threaten the material basis of Black life. The disparities in health care between whites and Blacks is adequately attested by the widening gap in life expectancy rates. American education is periodically deplored and condemned, and while there is exaggeration in the indictment, the condition of the resegregated schools of the nation is grim. The annual reports of the National Urban League on the State of Black America throughout the eighties and into the nineties offer all too poignant evidence of a great dream unfulfilled.

Above: After a successful term as Chairman of the National Committee of the Democratic Party, Ron Brown then accepted the bid of the Clinton administration to become Secretary of Commerce.

Below: Secretary for Veterans Affairs in the Clinton administration, Jesse Brown heads a vast agency which supervises hospitals, cemeteries, and vocational rehabilitation among its many other functions.

Public Life

One of the most expected outcomes of the Civil Rights Movement was to be the emphatic entrance of Blacks into mainstream political activity as voters and as officials. That fulfilment has been modest. The number of Blacks in the United States Congress in the House of Representatives, most of whom participate in the activities of the Black Caucus, has passed twenty, but by the end of 1992 there was only one Black in the Senate, nor were there many other viable candidates on the horizon. Only one Black has become governor of a state. As the inner cities and their deteriorating infrastructure have been abandoned to Blacks, a number have become mayors. Early on Cleveland, Atlanta, and Los Angeles elected Black mayors; and later Philadelphia, Baltimore, and New York City followed suit.

In other government areas there have been occasional Black cabinet officers and agency heads, and a number of diplomatic appointments, the high point in this area being reached during the administration of Democratic President Jimmy Carter, although the new Clinton regime looks promising. Clearly, the most spectacular figure in the executive branch, however, has been General Colin Powell, briefly National Security Advisor under President Ronald Reagan and Chairmain of the Joint Chiefs of Staff under Presidents George Bush and Bill Clinton.

In the pre-Civil Rights era, the distinguished Judge William Hastie was a lonely beacon of promise of the participation of Blacks in the federal judiciary. Beginning in the sixties, a number of outstanding appointments to the judiciary were made,

Above: In 1992, Carol Moseley Braun of Illinois made history by becoming the first African American woman ever elected to the United States Senate.

Right: Four-star General Colin Powell capped a distinguished military career by becoming Chairman of the Joint Chiefs of Staff of the United States Armed Forces.

notable those of Judge Constance Baker Motley and of Judge Leon Higginbottom, as well as the much-applauded appointment of Thurgood Marshall to the Supreme Court, after first serving as Solicitor General.

The Carter administration saw a considerable number of court appointments, most of high caliber. Twelve years of profoundly ideological tampering with the judiciary began with the Reagan administration and reached its apogee under Bush with the cynical nomination of an alleged successor to Marshall, the ultimate fallout of which sullied the Senate and, for better or worse, damages the image of the court for the foreseeable future. There is a cruel irony in a Black appointee having been the agent of the fiasco.

The change in the social and political atmosphere signaled by the election of Bill Clinton in November 1992 was palpable. The reversal of many of the policies and strategies undertaken by the right-wing ideologues (by far less genial than the Presidents whom they served), and which had cast such a pall on the aspirations and expectations of African Americans, seemed fated for modification and reversal. The lack of geniality that had characterized the governing elite had communicated itself to the country at large with a consequent deepening and widening of the racial divide.

Clinton seemed to offer not merely a new approach to the economy, which was tottering from the failed Reagan supply-side revolution, but also a politics of inclusion that was welcomed by the majority of African Americans, and by other excluded and harassed over-lapping minority groups of society, such as artists, homosexuals, women's groups, and environmentalists.

African Diaspora

The awareness of the African Diaspora and dispersion of sub-Saharan Blacks around the globe, but particularly in the Western Hemisphere, has its roots in the awareness of Africa itself, never absent in the consciousness of Black Americans from the beginning of their history. A particular instance of this was the presence of Du Bois and other Blacks at the Pan-African Conference of 1900 in London. Du Bois' own series of Pan-African Congresses from 1919 to 1928 captured this sensibility for intellectuals, while the Garvey Movement, with its overriding theme of African redemption, did so for a much larger public.

The theme of African continuities among Western Hemisphere Blacks provided another phase in the expansion of Diaspora consciousness. Writing in the 1920s on the spiritual, both James Weldon Johnson and R. Nathaniel Dett made claims for African continuity in this genre against the assertions of some white scholars. It was a white scholar, however, Melville Herskovits, who drew together a range of documentation in *The Myth of the Negro Past* (1940), and a leading Black sociologist, E. Franklin Frazier, who expressed his reservations.

A few Latin American scholars had preceded Herskovits in the exploration of African continuities in their respective domains, particularly Dr Jean Price-Mars in Haiti, and Fernando Ortiz in Cuba. Herskovits drew heavily on the linguistic work of the Black American Lorenzo Don Turner, who pioneered in Gullah studies.

Above: From his early career as a youthful civil rights leader to his present leadership role in the House of Representatives, John Lewis has been characterized by commitment to human values and human rights.

Below: As Mayor of New York, David Dinkins won people's respect, though he was beset by a nightmare of simultaneous financial, bureaucratic, and human deterioration.

In the Trans-African epoch, teaching and research on the African Diaspora is widespread and is the object of popular and frequently confused interests. Among Black academics who have been active in this area are St Clair Drake, John Henrik Clarke, Joseph E. Harris, Ruth Simms Hamilton, and Richard A. Long. White academics who have contributed significantly to Diaspora studies are Robert Farris Thompson, John Szwed, and Roger Abrahams.

Negritude and Beyond

In Paris in the early and mid-thirties, the common concerns of a group of student intellectuals from the far-flung French colonial empire gave rise to the movement called Negritude, the outstanding figures of which were Aimé Cesaire, Léon Dumas, and Léopold Sedar Senghor, all later to achieve distinction as poets and statesmen. As students, they were all aware of the Harlem Renaissance, and venerated Du Bois, Alain Locke, and Langston Hughes. They were also in direct contact with Black American academics such as Mercer Cook and E.A. Jones.

Following World War II, the Society of African Culture, ably directed by Alione Diop, emerged from the Negritude Movement, and issued the important cultural journal *Présence Africaine*, which for a while appeared in English and French. Its range and readership have encompassed Africa and the Diaspora. The Society of African Culture held a Conference of Black Writers and Scholars in Paris in 1956, and a later one in Rome. Black Americans participating in the Paris conference organized the American Society of African Culture, and in that capacity directed American par-

ticipation in the crowning event of Negritude, the First World Festival of Black and Negro Arts held in Dakar, Senegal in 1966. Senghor was then President of Senegal and Mercer Cook the United States Ambassador to the country. Prominent among the participating Black Americans were Langston Hughes, Katherine Dunham, Duke Ellington, and the Alvin Ailey American Dance Theatre. The subsequent Colloquium on Negritude held in Dakar in 1971 and the frequently postponed Festival of the African World held in Nigeria in 1977 added little to the luster of the Dakar Festival.

The Black Power thrust in the Civil Rights Movement in the mid-sixties was paralleled by analogous tendencies in the arts and in religious studies, two important axes of Black American life.

More politically focused and doctrinaire than Negritude, the Black Aesthetic, celebrated in a collection of that title edited by Addison Gayle (1971), lay at the heart of the Black Arts Movement. The leading critic associated with the Black Aesthetic was Hoyt Fuller, editor of *Negro Digest* which was later renamed *Black World*. Fuller actively encouraged young writers through a workshop, OBAC (Organization of Black American Culture), and visual artists through AFRICOBRA (African Commune of Black Relevant Artists), a collective headed by Jeff Donaldson. *Black Arts and Black Aesthetics* (1981), a bibliography by Carolyn Fowler, offers useful documentation of the movement.

While the stridency of the Black Aesthetic authors and critics has subsided, the rise of a new cultural criticism, rooted in studies of literature and folklore, may be considered its

Above: After an early triumph on TV's *Saturday Night Live*, Eddie Murphy became the comedy star of a succession of successful Hollywood blockbuster films.

Below: Oprah Winfrey has become synonymous with exciting and arresting "real life" television. Her personality has conquered the public in the United States, Canada and the United Kingdom.

Above: Arsenio Hall entered the world of late-night TV shows and carved out a considerable niche with his ethnically based hip style.

185

Above: An inspired actress, Whoopi Goldberg has displayed her comic and dramatic gifts in a number of films, winning an Oscar for her role as a medium in *Ghosts*.

Right: As host of the *Today Show*, Bryant Gumbel occupies an important position in America's media landscape.

Below: Jessye Norman is a remarkably versatile singer, who is equally at home in French and German opera and art song as in classics of the American musical stage and the spiritual.

Facing page: In his meteoric career in film, Spike Lee has emerged as a great talent and a lightning rod for controversy.

legacy. An outstanding figure in this area is Henry Louis Gates, Jr. who has been prolific as critic and editor. Others in this multifaceted domain are Houston Baker, Eleanor Traylor, and Hortense Spillers.

A Black perspective in religion may be perceived to have its roots in the theology of the late nineteenth century A.M.E. Bishop, Henry McNeal Turner. From the late thirties, the eloquent Howard Thurman – in his preaching and meditative writings – sought to add the insight of the spiritual to Christian "disciplines and resources." It was the book *Black Theology* (1969) by James Cone, however, which signaled a ferment in the examination of Christianity from the perspective of the Black experience, and initiated a wide range of scholarship and action in this domain.

Media

While many tendencies and movements among Black Americans have demarcated divergences and contrasts, both inherent and imposed, from the mainstream, the electronic media, film, audio and visual recordings, and television often provide striking examples of convergence toward the mainstream. Paradoxically, however, divergence also emerges in the media.

Since the eighties, two of the most visible media figures in the United States, and elsewhere, have been television personalities Bill Cosby and Oprah Winfrey, he in a situation comedy series and she in the problem-focused talk show. Black news and events anchors, both male and female, are found from coast to coast, and on the national scene, Bryant Gumbel and Bernard Shaw are household names. Television is

also the prime vehicle of the video recording, which brings such performing artists as Whitney Houston and Michael Jackson to millions worldwide. From the ethnic-oriented, frequently contentious, genre of rap, television has gleaned an international crossover star, the anodyne Hammer.

The situation in the feature film world is more complex, for most films continue to present and, some assert, to preserve, the racially compartmentalized nature of American life. Nevertheless, the actors Whoopi Goldberg and Eddie Murphy have both conquered a wide public, and the filmmaker Spike Lee has managed to evoke a great deal of admiration and antipathy while achieving a widely recognized success.

It is not too much to declare that Black representation in the media, America's major conduit to the world, provides a microcosm of the tensions and complexities of Black American life at the end of the twentieth century.

Clinton's Inauguration

No greater testimony to the power of electronic media could be cited than that provided by the intense coverage of the inauguration of Bill, now William Jefferson, Clinton. While African Americans had been barely visible, except as spectators, at the inaugurations of his two predecessors, their presence at the Clinton inauguration was emphatic. The symbolism of this occasion was not lost on African Americans, on their fellow countrymen, or on a watching and tortured world.

Notably, Clinton requested that their choir of Philander Smith College of Little Rock, Arkansas, sing at the occasion, and he turned to poet

Above: For years, Hollywood's sole Black leading man, Sidney Poitier has been a great inspiration to all his colleagues in the performing arts.

Right: Whitney Houston is a well-regarded popular singing star who is credited with a succession of mega hits.

Facing page: Television comedian, paterfamilias and quiz master, Bill Cosby is also an author, a philanthropist, and a collector of art and antiques.

Below: Though the image of rap music has been tarnished by unfortunate charges of obscenity, the decorous M.C. Hammer is the most highly rewarded and acclaimed personality of the genre.

Facing page, far right: Wilfred Delphin and Edwin Romain perform to critical acclaim a large repertory of piano literature ranging from Mozart to Scott Joplin.

Maya Angelou, reared in Stamps, Arkansas, for an inaugural poem. Her appearance signaled inclusion – a woman, an African American, a poet, an artist, a college professor.

The concluding stanzas of the Angelou poem, *On the Pulse of Morning*, were:

The horizon leans forward,
Offering you space to place new
   steps of change.
Here, on the pulse of this fine day
You may have the courage
To look up and out and upon me,
   the
Rock, the River, the Tree, your
   country.
No less to Midas than the
   mendicant.
No less to you now than the
   mastodon then.

Here, on the pulse of this new
   day
You may have the grace to look
   up and out
And into your sister's eyes, and
   into
Your brother's face, your country
And say simply
With hope –
Good morning.

Index

Picture Credits

Allsport 4, 167, 172, 174–5, 177–9 **Hulton Deutsch Collection** 74–5, 90, 150 Bettmann Archive 1, 12–13, 23, 30, 31, 35, 37, 38, 44, 49, 51, 54, 56–7 bottom, 60, 64, 67, 102 top, 129, 130, 133, 138–9, 140–1, 155, 160–1, 162, 164, 165, 168 right, 170, 173 top Consolidated 181, 182, left, 184 bottom, 185 bottom, 188 bottom left Empics 171 bottom left S.I. 185 top, 186 top left, 187 left **Colorific!** 101, 106, 168 left Black Star 88–9 Wheeler Pictures 114 **Creative Cartography Limited** 1985 8 **Image Bank** Charles W. Bush 171 Lawrence Fried 107 H. de Lespinasse 134–5 **Richard Long** 39, 66, 115 **London Features International** 142, 152 right **MacClancy Collection** 20 bottom, 34 **Multimedia Research** 40–42, 57 top, 58–9, 63, 65, 69–71, 73, 78, 110, 112, 117, 122–4, 126, 158 **NBC** 186 right **Peter Newark's Western Americans** 9–11, 16–19, 20 top, 21, 24–6, 29, 32, 33, 36, 45–8, 52, 55, 80–83, 99 top, 163, 166, 169 **David Redfern** 50, 53, 125, 128, 131, 132, 137, 143–9, 151, 152 left **Rex Features** E. Adebari 153 P. Brooker 173 bottom Krug 186 left LGI Daphne 103 LGI L. Goldsmith 189 left Sipa Bob Black Chicago Sun-Times 182 right Sipa Kuss 100 Sipa Colin 176 Sipa Mircovich 188 right Sipa Trippett 183 C. Sykes 180 **Joanne Rile Artists' Management** 189 right **Susan J. Ross** 116 top left, 159 bottom left, 184 top, 188 top **Frank Spooner Pictures** 111, 154 Gamma 102 bottom **Topham Picture Library** 76–7, 84–7, 91–8, 99 bottom, 104–5, 157 **Virago** 113 **The Whitney Museum of American Art** 118–121 **Valerie Wilmer** 79, 136.